BETWEEN THE SHELVES

A TRIBUTE TO LIBRARIES
by Edmonton Writers

Edited by Hal J. Friesen & Brad OH Inc.

Between the Shelves:
A Tribute to Libraries by Edmonton Writers
Copyright © 2015

All individual contributions are copyright
by their respective authors.

Edited by Hal J. Friesen & Brad OH Inc.
Interior Design by Hal J. Friesen
Cover Art & Design by Debbie Ha

ISBN: 1508469814
ISBN-13: 978-1508469810

FIRST EDITION

Printed by CreateSpace

CONTENTS

Acknowledgements...i

Introduction
Hal J. Friesen & Brad OH Inc..1

The Library
Timothy Fowler..3

Neve Uncovers the Ultimate Truth of All Things
Brad OH Inc..7

Bakster's Proposition
Mark Parsons...22

Five Hundred Years
T. K. Boomer..36

The Turning of a Page
Brian Clark...42

Melvil Dui Conquers All
Vivian Zenari... 48

I Will Not Let You Fall
Linda Webber..69

Library Lost
M. L. Kulmatycki..75

Learning From Your Library
Mohamed Abdi...100

Newcomers to Canada and Edmonton Public Libraries
TrudieAberdeen..118

Reading After Hours
Hal J. Friesen..128

Acknowledgements

Thanks go out to Michael Sweetman for some last-minute consultation, and to Debbie Ha for doing such a fantastic job on the cover.

Introduction

The Edmonton Writers' Group (EWG) began as a Romance Writers' Group and gradually evolved to include creators from all genres. Throughout its decade-plus history, the group has been hosted in meeting rooms at various locations of the Edmonton Public Libraries (EPL). Therefore it is no stretch to say that the EWG owes its existence to the EPL, and it is partly in recognition of the important role of local libraries that the group's members have contributed to this anthology. All of the proceeds of this book's sales will go toward supporting the EWG's birthplace, the library.

The stunning array of services the EPL offers is only a small fraction of the power that libraries can have in the life and sustenance of a community. Each and every piece in this anthology offers a different perspective and taste on the theme of what libraries bring to humanity. From the archival role of Mr. Dewey's decimal system, to a place to calm life's chaos, to important cultural stitching and mending, and even into the far future, the results will shed light far beyond the obvious. Each of the pieces informed and touched us editors, and we hope they do the same for you.

-Hal J. Friesen & Brad OH Inc.

The Library

by Timothy Fowler

When not writing for Scribbles and Snaps, Tim works with a Global Fortune 100, leading a team of incredibly talented people to deliver the nearly impossible to their customers doing important work. He travels nearly full time as a result of this engagement, and part time for leisure. He scribbles pictures and snaps stories for his own pleasure and hopefully yours. He lives in St. Albert with his lovely wife, Saskatchewan-born farm girl, Kathy, and Gordon Setter, Rigby. He is Scribbler, Snapper, Navigator, Outdoorsman, Fellow Traveller. He is from Granite Rockies, and Prairie Dust, from Boreal Forest and Wanderlust.

Tweet @TimothyDFowler or read his blog at www.scribblesandsnaps.

Today I signed up for membership at our local library. On my way home, memories of my childhood library bubbled up. I feel a lifetime of pleasure in hard covered books as I recall clumps of root-bound amethyst the size of watermelons placed carefully, like magic crystals, at the foot of round side-tables covered in green brocade draped to the floor and solid wood doors stretching to the ceiling. The smell of exotic food cooking somewhere in the house sneaks in with these memories. Was it the food or the library at my Aunt and Uncle's house that made it feel luxurious? She was a dress designer, he a chef. Both were hoteliers. Who today has a room in their house dedicated to books? They had a library then, and I do now, complete luxury.

I recall sitting in the big chair, bathed in the warm evening light with the weight of books that took all the strength of my little-boy hands to remove from the shelf and onto my lap. I remember the weight of those books balanced on my knees, the satiny feel of good paper and the smell of old leather-bound books. In the background, I can smell preparations for a celebratory dinner underway. I hear adult conversation wafting down the hall. The exotic aromas from the kitchen were the only real distraction in the library.

Books hold complex layers of appeal. Vivid images pop in my head and the collection of letters speak as if put together specifically for me. The author's voice seemed to know me better than anyone. Sometimes I imagined casting glances over my shoulder to make sure no one was secretly watching me, the experience of being lost in books so real.

That library became sacred to me, the words too. In time, the library moved, gone with my Aunt and Uncle, but the wonder remained. The special connection across time and space that puzzled and intrigued continues today.

The trip to the local library felt like a return to my Aunt and Uncle's. I could almost smell caramelized roast from the book covers. When I got home with my new library card, I felt an immense sense of satisfaction, almost smugness. Where else can you get access to thousands of books for just twenty dollars a year? Even better, the books are now much easier to get on my lap, and I can carry more than one at a time.

I found and then invited home Joyce, Faulkner and

King for an intimate conversation. Each one with something special to say, holding so much potential between the bindings. I lost track of time while searching, thumbing, reading and luxuriating in all those books.

Books are much of my life experience, adding richness and complexity, and sometimes simplicity and humour. As a kid, books allowed me to escape the backseat of the car on family road trips, allowing me to have mini travel adventures of my very own. As a teen, books taught me how to repair bicycles, motorcycles and, eventually, cars. As an adult I consulted books to address management issues, solve parenting challenges and help untangle sticky life situations. I even followed Robert Ludlum and others down the escape hatch to an alternate reality for a break from whatever I faced.

A fresh book cracked on my lap made the bus ride to my downtown office more productive and enjoyable. Later on when traveling in earnest, I read on planes commuting to interprovincial responsibilities. Every now and then, I get a gentle poke for reading too much 'serious' stuff. Occasionally fiction makes its way onto my bookshelf. There are serious things to learn there too. Now I read books about the craft of writing, how to get published and about proper language usage.

We took our boys at an early age to the library. Most evenings wound down on the couch, after a bath, with a favourite book. We found ourselves weekly at the library. I recall the bug-eyed amazement as they stuffed books in their backpacks for the trek home. The wonder I saw on their faces reflects an image of my own when I was their age.

"Really Dad, we can take all these books home for free?" they would say.

As a new grandpa I experience the pleasure again. My granddaughter selects a special book from the bottom shelf in our library. That lowest shelf holds some of the books from when I was a child and some of her father's books. I hope the magic of words and the author's voice speak to her. The look on her face says she hears the special voice too.

Stephen King, in his book on the craft of writing, refers to writing as telepathy. Authors, some dead for centuries, send messages across time and space—in books. Thinking about the writers from years ago speaking to me now from that place, I am humbled and impressed by the magnitude of the literature available at the library. Our library.

Now I am back in my big chair, the weight of the borrowed books on my lap, stirring me, returning to the magical place that books transport us to: the land of amethyst, soft light, easy conversation and exquisite pleasure. I feel the urge to look over my shoulder.

Neve Uncovers the Ultimate Truth of All Things

by Brad OH Inc.

Brad OH Inc. is a thought conglomerate consisting primarily of Brad OH, who is based out of Edmonton, Alberta. Brad OH has a background in psychology, with a philosophy minor. Brad OH Inc. writes with the intention of entertaining, while drawing attention to a variety of social and interpersonal quandaries. The Brad OH Inc. blog can be found at http://bradohinc.com, and includes both posts and short stories, as well as information about his upcoming novel, 'Edgar's Worst Sunday'.

Book shelves rose up like forbidden towers on old castles, meandering off in every direction. Neve, caressing the stringy and stained hair of her doll Clarice, bit her tiny lip. She could hear the lackadaisical clicking of the keyboard behind her as her father continued his arduous journey to find new employment. She knew it wasn't going well. It never did.

Neve was always getting dragged along to the library for his half-hearted attempts to turn things around, and was expected to wait nearby as her dad perused the net in search of employment. Her family didn't have Internet at their house. 'That was for those rich...' well, Neve really didn't like to say bad words, and reasoned that thinking them probably counted just as much.

Still, waiting around like this was a tall task. Neve was only eight, after all.

"What do you think we should do, Clarice?" she whispered, hoping to avoid any dirty looks or shushes from the library's other patrons. But her doll just stared back with her one button-eye, providing little by way of answer. Neve was too old to be talking to dolls anyway, she figured.

'Yet not old enough to have other fun,' she thought.

"Neve! Quit wandering around so much. Stay where I can see you," her dad barked. His eyes never left the screen, which cast a deathly pallor over his already exhausted face.

"Yeah, yeah," she mumbled to herself, imagining Clarice's button-eye rolling back to mirror her own. Neve had never been a disobedient child, but the library was pretty familiar to her after so many months of this routine, and that meant the temptation to drift away was nearly overwhelming her eager young mind.

The small cluster of computers where her dad sat was stationed in the very centre of the library—an oasis of desks and screens enveloped by a world of wonder. About two person-lengths from the computers in all directions, the tall rows of bookshelves rolled away into distances Neve couldn't even imagine. One way led to fantasy books, where Neve could find old tales about knights and dragons. Beside that was non-fiction, which had never really captured Neve. Then there were the young-adult, horror, and literature sections. Yuck, yikes, and yawn! But just to her right was the row for science fiction books. There, Neve knew, she could read about unimaginable alien worlds, and starships piloted by people totally foreign in their experiences, yet somehow unbearably familiar in their struggles.

Neve liked that section a lot. Once, she recalled, she'd flipped through a book with pictures of giant space stations, and terrible battles in the stars. There had even been a princess in distress—just like in so many of the fantasy stories Neve loved.

Pulling Clarice tightly to her chest, Neve eyed the countless pathways eagerly. She was a good reader for her age—even her teacher, Mrs. MacNeil, had said so on a sticker covered certificate which now hung on Neve's bedroom wall. So her regular trips to the library had grown bolder bit by bit, and whenever her dad was sufficiently distracted, she would wander a little further down one row or another, reading anything she could get her hands on.

She turned in tiny circles as she thought about the possibilities. The spinning made her dizzy, but Neve didn't mind. "That way is where the romance books are," she told Clarice—as if the doll didn't already know. Over the last couple of months, Neve and Clarice had been nearly permanent fixtures in their local library branch. "I like those ones," she purred quietly to her little stuffed friend, and felt a flush creeping into her cheeks.

Neve remembered one book in particular. She'd flipped through it on one of her first trips to the library, struggling with some of the words and wishing for pictures, but doing very well on the whole, according to Clarice. The book had been an old story about star-crossed lovers separated by cruel circumstances. No matter what they did, their paths just never seemed to bring them together.

Neve liked how they never gave up hope though.

Clutching the rough cover in her little hands, she'd hoped her parents held onto that same hope.

"Books can be a big help to people, you know."

Clarice only gaped at Neve's prompt, but this didn't stop her. Once, Mrs. MacNeil had said Neve was 'headstrong'. One trip to the library later, Neve learned that meant she didn't quit when things got tough. That had made her happy.

"Just remember the woman we met in the 'Religion' section?" she continued.

The memory from several weeks ago still remained with Neve, fighting tenaciously for space amongst confounding math problems, cruel playground rumours, and half-comprehended speculations from her dad about where they were going to live.

Neve had been standing at the threshold of the aisle, inching in slowly as she kept one vigilant eye on her dad. The covers seemed scary, with blood and fire and thorns. Neve had actually begun to wonder if she'd stumbled into the horror section again by accident, when she saw the short old lady holding a light purple book. She had tears running down her face, and Neve's strong sense of sympathy had overpowered her aversion to scoldings.

"What's wrong?" she asked, staring up at the frail blue-haired lady.

The woman was startled at first, but her expression naturally softened when she saw Clarice. "Oh, oh bless your heart. Nothing's wrong my dear. I was just reading an old passage that my mother used to read to me. I never understood it back then," she explained with a paper-thin smile before being interrupted by a gross coughing fit. She put a hand to her chest, and her old body shook. "It speaks to me now though," she finished, and creaked slowly away, leaning upon her rocker.

With an emboldened spirit, Neve had picked up the book and flipped through it. There were a lot of lines about valleys, and fear, and other things Neve didn't really understand. But she remembered how much it had meant to the lady.

Now, Neve could still hear the slow clicking of the keyboard, and a quick glance backward told her that her dad remained fixated on his own quest.

With one tentative step, then another, Neve inched her way into the fantasy section, where the book covers showed horses and dragons and all sorts of wonderful scenes. Picking up a pale green book with a white sword on it, Neve flipped the pages excitedly, her mind a maelstrom of big ideas and vague hopes.

Foreign words were scattered freely throughout the text, but many of them were pretty close to words she knew, and the clever girl was able to make some general sense from the lines she read as she flipped happily through the pages. There had been a king long ago, in a land that had a new name now. The king had a sword.

"Not just any sword," she whispered to Clarice, whose little grey button eye seemed to wobble with excitement, "a magic sword, pulled from a stone! It's what makes him king, but..." Neve paused, considering what a hard time the king seemed to be having.

She flipped a few pages, searching for the happy parts. She'd looked through the book a dozen times before—

sometimes she felt like she'd done so with every book in the library. Inevitably though, she'd find something new with each venture into the forbidding stacks.

"The sword is why he's king, but he can never figure out how to make the people happy. He gets advice from a wizard, and he listens to his people, but everyone wants something different." Neve felt silly sometimes, whispering to a doll. But someone had to share in these adventures with her. She was pretty sure that was a rule.

"I think it's hard to be good sometimes, Clarice. Sometimes there's no way to make everyone happy, and—"

"Neve, get back here!" her dad's voice ricocheted across the library, and people stared at Neve, many with long bony fingers pressed to their thin gray lips. "How many times do I have to tell you?"

"Sorry dad." Neve hurried back to his side, her eyes glued to the faded blue carpet. "I was just reading about a—"

"That's OK honey, just don't wander too far." He never looked away from the screen.

"Hmmph." Neve flopped down onto the floor beside the computer desk, her eyebrows bunched tightly together. There was a garbage can next to her, but a quick peek in revealed nothing but bunched up papers and a few cough drop wrappers. The floor was mostly clean.

Neve looked at the clock, trying to follow the second hand around its course, but that got boring after only a few rotations.

"This is taking forever," she whined, and Clarice nodded her emphatic support. She picked lackadaisically at the flaking paint on the leg of the computer table, but didn't like the way it scraped under her fingernails. "Hmmph."

On the shelf closest to her, Neve could see a big hard-cover book with pictures of stars and planets and comets and crazy glowing balls of purple light and lots of other things she didn't understand.

It didn't seem that far away. A quick glance up to her dad told Neve he was still fixated by…whatever it was he looked at.

She lay down on the floor. Keeping one toe pressed firmly against her dad's workstation as instructed, she stretched out on her stomach, her tiny fingers reaching out for the big old book.

"Darn, not quite enough," she grumbled.

Her eyes flashed about like fireflies, desperately trying to figure out a way to reach the book, which hovered just a few inches beyond her grasp. But there was no way to stretch any farther without running the risk of tearing her skeleton loose from her skin, and Neve certainly didn't want to do that. Her back was already getting sore, and she relaxed her posture a bit. No one was going to help her; that much was certainly clear.

With sudden clairvoyance, Neve reached the only deci-sion available to her, and quickly chucked poor Clarice at the book, knocking it down from the shelf with a loud 'Whop!'

A gale of 'Shushes' flooded her ears as she was buried under a tsunami of dirty looks. "Neve, be quiet. Don't you get that we're in a library?" her dad snapped.

Neve scooped up the book—and Clarice—with her toes still grounded firmly against the desk, and shimmied giddily back. Success!

Sitting up with her back against the hard old desk leg, she nestled the heavy book in her lap, placed Clarice comfortably in view just above it, and opened it up.

Neve's mouth hung open as she took in the incredible, double-page panoramas. Tremendous clusters of stars spread out before her; entire galaxies scattered over the blackness like spilled marbles, and foreign planets beyond count were pictured within.

She gasped. "It's all so big!" Scrunching up closer to the desk leg, Neve held her breath as she flipped the pages. She remembered again the lady she'd spoken to in the religion section, and how moved she'd been by what she was reading. "There's something for everyone here I guess. There's certainly room for it," she finished, flipping the pages eagerly.

With such a humongous universe out there, it seemed nearly impossible that there could be any certain answers to all the strange things people wondered; just an ever-expanding list of questions. Neve pulled Clarice closer as she read about how all the stars she could see in the night sky existed in only an itsy-bitsy little portion of their single galaxy.

"It sure makes you feel small, doesn't it?"

"You still there, baby?" her dad asked from just above her. It sounded like a world away.

"I'm still here Daddy," she answered quietly.

Neve had a lot of questions herself: Who would she play with at recess tomorrow? Why wasn't she allowed to do anything by herself? What did her parents always used to fight about? Where was her mom anyways?

Looking at all the thousands of stars, and all the great

empty spaces between them, Neve realized that she'd kind of given up on getting answers for them anyway. 'But sometimes,' she thought, 'the stories here are even better. Answers don't seem so important when you have a good story, after all.'

Gazing at the big bright pages in amazement, Neve remembered another story she'd read once. She hadn't understood a lot of it, but she'd gotten bits and pieces. It was about an astronaut on a big spaceship, flying through the stars to discover…something.

She'd thought he must have been very lonely, drifting farther and farther from home all alone.

He did have a robot he could talk to, but it didn't really seem anxious to help him or make him feel better. It just wanted to do what needed to be done for the mission, and never cared what the poor astronaut needed for himself.

"Can't I go get another book, Daddy?" Neve asked.

"I'm afraid I can't let you do that, Neve. I've got to keep my eye on you, that's a dad's job after all," he replied. The façade of his cheery tone was entirely transparent to the whip-smart young Neve.

Neve slouched down, closing the big book in her lap and looking at Clarice. "That astronaut did his job, even though he had that stupid old robot to deal with. I guess I have to too," she declared. But Clarice didn't answer, and Neve tossed her down onto the floor.

She was too old to talk to dolls anyway. Doll didn't have brains like people. Clarice couldn't answer all the questions Neve had. Clarice couldn't talk or think or even ask questions for herself.

'No', Neve thought, 'only people can do that.'

She remembered another story she'd looked at once, sitting down next to her dad in the big old library. It was a long story, and there was a whole shelf in the library to hold all the books it took to tell it. She didn't get through very much, but flipping through the old yellow pages, taking in that happy, musty smell, she'd managed to catch enough.

It was a fantasy story, like so many others she'd read. It was about an amazing world full of beautiful elves and terrible goblins and all sorts of strange stuff like that. But the world was dying; all the magic was disappearing and all the good people were going away, leaving the world to darkness and decay.

It made her sad then, and it made her sad thinking about it now. She looked over at Clarice folded in half on the ground and sighed. "The people in that story didn't believe things could go back either, not to the way they used to be," she whispered down to her hopeless friend.

Neve blushed, but a quick glance up to her father revealed that he hadn't been listening—still absorbed in the cool blue glow of the screen in front of him.

'They'd still tried though,' she remembered that much at least. The smallest and most helpless had stood up to undo all the hurt, and carried the burden even though they couldn't possibly understand what it all really meant.

Neve liked that.

Sometimes as she read one book or another, she felt like it had been written just for her. It was weird, because that made her wonder how anyone else could possibly understand it, since they didn't know all the things she knew. But they did understand. Everyone found something in those books, and that's what made them so great.

"Only people can ask questions, and only people can imagine answers." Neve sighed, and pulled Clarice back over to her side. 'It must be easy,' she thought, 'to be a doll and only worry about doll things: How you sit on the bed, what dress to wear—those things are easy-as-pie.' Other than her one missing button-eye, Clarice had the best life Neve could imagine. And the missing button-eye didn't even seem to bother Clarice.

Clutching the doll tightly in one hand now, she imagined the tiny weight was unbearable, just like the magic ring in the book she'd read. She crawled slowly; dragging Clarice along the worn carpet, fearing that at any moment the watchful eye of her father would settle upon her and end their adventure before it even began.

But no scolding came, and Neve slipped silently away into the aisle marked 'Classics'.

She'd been here before too, so she took no time at all locating her favourite book. There was a silly drawing of a naked yellow man on the cover, and Neve had to bite her little lip to suppress a giggle. She had to do that every time.

The man seemed to be drawn on a pot, but Neve could never figure out what that had to do with the stories—which were all about the ancient gods of Greece, and the strange games they played with people.

Sometimes, Neve wondered if that's how Clarice felt—manipulated against her will by a giant girl she could barely comprehend. That made Neve feel awfully powerful, and every time the thought entered her mind, she vowed to ensure she treated Clarice with all the respect she wanted for herself.

The gods in these stories weren't like that though. Not at all. They killed and tortured their people, and gave them impossible labours to do, and then punished them if they did any of it wrong.

It all seemed so unfair.

Neve peeked around the corner to make sure her dad hadn't caught on to her absence. He'd be awfully mad if she didn't sit still in the place where she was told. But he just gazed at his screen, oblivious and fully occupied with whatever worried adults.

She flipped through the book cautiously. She didn't want to stumble on some awful drawing again—once she'd seen one of a bird eating a man's guts, and that had put her off her thanksgiving dinner, which also made her dad angry. All the stories in this section were terribly gruesome. In fact, Neve had avoided the section for a long time after discovering what it contained, but eventually she grew curious, and finally began to visit it again.

At first, she couldn't understand why anyone would want to read something so awful. When she was younger, Neve only liked happy stories about beautiful princesses and magical times.

But at some point or another, those things began to feel a bit silly.

They were nice to imagine, and Neve still liked it when her dreams were happy, but she couldn't deny that sometimes she liked those darker stories. She wondered about the people who wrote them. Mrs. MacNeil had talked about the ancient Greeks once, and although Neve didn't know much, she knew they were from a time long, long ago. 'Probably even before Christopher Columbus,' she imagined.

"Why do you think they wrote those stories?" she whispered the question into the side of Clarice's stuffed, earless head. "Do you think they really thought that's what God was like, or do you think they just needed a way to blow off steam?"

One time, Mrs. MacNeil had sent Neve out of the classroom, and she had to sit down and talk about anger with the school counsellor. Neve was scared at first, but it turned out OK. She got to hold a big fluffy toy frog, which was nice, and they mostly just talked about things which made Neve mad—which somehow made her feel better about them.

In the end, the counsellor had told her to count to ten, and to drink some water, and to walk away. Neve didn't know how to do all those things together without making a big mess and getting in even more trouble though, so she didn't really bother. But she remembered that the counsellor had also told her how important it was to talk about it. She said you could talk to toys, or people you trust, or even write it down.

"That's probably what they were doing," Neve told Clarice, "just trying to write down all the things that scared them back then. That's really good to do, because once you write it down, it's not as scary anymore."

Neve thought about the diary she'd started once, back when everything first started to change. She'd written big stories about her dad and her mom and their old house, but it was really hard work, and she'd ultimately given up.

"Oh," said Neve, flipping through the thin pages with Clarice nestled snuggly in her lap, "this is one of my favourites." She turned the book upward to show Clarice the full-page picture of the stone man and his lion skin and his big muscles. Then she blushed, shook her head at Clarice, and pulled the book back up with a huff.

"This guy was the son of Zeus—the king of the gods. But Zeus's wife Hera didn't like him, and they always fought. He was tormented by Hera, who only showed up when she wanted to make things hard for him and drive him crazy.

"But he never gave up. Sometimes he used his strength, and sometimes he used his brains, but he never gave up. I think that's pretty important.

"I wonder who wrote this story," said Neve, searching through the covers and end-pages for some kind of 'about the author' section.

"Neve!" The yell sent a chill up her spine.

The jig was up!

"Neve, get back here!" her dad called again. "You know better than to wander off. It's time to go. C'mon!"

Sinking down against the rigid bookshelf, Neve frowned. 'Time to go home,' she thought. That meant a lot of things: It meant that bedtime was near for one thing, and dreams were always sort of a gamble. It also meant a whole day of school; wandering the halls alone and hoping someone would talk to her. She hated that!

Hopefully though, her dad would need to do more work tomorrow, because that would mean she'd get to come back here. She looked forward to being at the library. At any moment, some story could take her to a world she'd never heard of but always needed.

It amazed her how familiar they always felt.

"Neve! Let's go. Now!"

"Well Clarice, it's time to go," she said, replacing the book on the shelf and gently taking her doll up by the hand. "I still think it's unfair sometimes that people are the only ones who have to wonder why. It hurts to have so many questions. But I've gotta admit—I'm glad we have imaginations. At least that way, when we don't know all the real answers, we can think up something that makes sense, right Clarice?"

"That's right," said Clarice, her voice as smooth and comforting as a mother's touch. "I think we're going to be just fine, Neve."

Bakster's Proposition

by Mark Parsons

Mark Parsons has been curled up in coffee shop corners, scratching furiously in his notebook since 2004. He has several projects on the go, including *Fire & Flesh* (Fantasy), *The Silent Dark Pentalogy* (Science Fiction), and *Brothers* (Non-Fiction). "Bakster's Proposition" is his first short story.

J ohn looked up from his steaming coffee as he heard his wife Kelly push open the front door with her shoulder, her purse dangling from her arm. He couldn't see her from the kitchen, but he could hear her mood as her purse hit the floor, followed by a 'flump' on the sofa.

"How was your trip to the library?" he asked, knowing the answer. Kelly's words were muffled by the couch, but her tone was not. "That good, huh?"

Kelly pushed herself up from the couch. Simon, the Momma's Boy of their five cats, jumped up on Kelly's lap and started purring. "The building I entered today might be called 'The Library' by the local yokels, but it's a far cry from anything back home."

John carried his mug to the couch and sat next to Kelly. She slid into his shoulder as Simon stretched out and then curled up between them. "I've seen a bigger selection of books at a gas station."

"Well, there's only what, 50 people in this town?" John said, scratching Simon under his orange and white chin. "This is why we moved here, isn't it? To get away from everything? We knew that things would be different. I wouldn't expect them to have the complete works of Tolstoy—the nearest college is 100 miles away!"

"Yes," Kelly said with a loud exhale, "but I would hope that a library has at least one creative work of art. It was more like a walk-in encyclopedia. They had every single Farmer's Almanac dating back to 1792, but they didn't have 'The Cat in the Hat'!" Kelly let her head roll back on the couch and puffed at a strand of her red hair that fell across her face. "What do we do?"

John furrowed his brow mid-sip. He swallowed thickly. "What do you mean?"

"I mean we have to fix this, right? These heathens need to have a proper library."

"Kelly, this isn't the cultural Mecca of the mid-West. This is Grayfield, Alberta—we aren't even on the map! Listen, we only moved here a week ago. Can we at least wait until we've been here a month before we start rocking the boat?"

Kelly let out a frustrated sigh.

"Johnathan Bakster, I love you dearly, but you can be such a bastard when you're right. I miss the libraries from back home. The comforting smell of the glue that holds the pages together; the weight of the old anthologies; the sight of children curled in the corner, mouth agape, wondering if their hero would escape evil. Before I met you, John, I would visit the library on my way home from work and just breathe in knowledge. There is something magical and rejuvenating about a library. Well, a proper library, that is. Apparently there is some law here where the books can't out-number the citizens."

John leaned in and caressed the side of Kelly's face with his hand. She placed her hand over his, letting the warmth of his touch relax her thoughts.

"Promise me you'll wait until after Canada Day before you try and change the world?" John laughed to himself. "My dear sweet Kelly. I love you with all of my heart, but I also know when to get out of your way. Canada Day is just over a month away—that's plenty of time to figure out how to bring some culture to this town."

* * *

"Do you need a hand, John?"

"No, baby, I'm good!" John grimaced as he was finally able to pull his easel out through the back door. He knew he should have traded it for a smaller one back home before they moved, but John was convinced that there would be a place to buy one in Grayfield. After a month of asking around, he found out the few who did have one had it passed down through the family. Oh well, it was cumbersome but solid. "I haven't seen the boys since I got home. Are they out?"

Kelly sat up straight and wiped the dirt and sweat from her brow with her arm. "Simon and Teddie are out some-where." She sighed, turning to face John. "Usually they stay close and help me garden, but today they are on a wild adventure. How was work today?"

"Same-ol' same ol'." John grunted as he set the massive easel down in a corner of the backyard. "Me trying to learn how things are done in small towns while struggling to convince people to move into the 21st Century. Showed them something I threw together in Photoshop and I thought Steve was going to have a heart attack. How about you?" John looked at the ground around him, remembered he left his paints inside, and jogged back towards the house.

"My day was wonderful! Ann-Marie is such a wonderful manager. I'm glad she's taken such a liking to me and my business ideas. She figures I'll be managing partner by the end of the year."

John came back out with his paints and set them down by his easel when he heard their front gate open and close.

"Hello, hello!"

"Oh hi Bernadette, please let yourself in." John's sarcasm earned him a sideways glare from Kelly. "How can we help you?"

"Oh I just came by to say that I think what you're doing is great!" she proclaimed, putting her hands on her hips. Simon and Teddie came back and started purring and rubbing up against Bernadette. Kelly said they liked her because she has cats as well, but John was convinced that it had to do more with her being the town Wiccan.

"Oh it's nothing special," replied John, "just trying to get by like anyone else."

"No, I mean your Motion for the Town Hall meeting—that's the only way to get anything done around here!" Bernadette declared, smiling.

"Why, yes. Of course. The meeting." John turned to Kelly who refused to return his gaze. "We can't wait!" John turned back to Bernadette with a fake smile.

"OK, well, see you there!" As she turned, Simon and Teddie went to follow her, but Kelly called them back.

John cut her off. "When were you going to tell me?"

"Tomorrow."

"When is the town hall?"

"...tomorrow..." Kelly paused. "Are you mad at me?"

John took a deep breath. "I'm disappointed you didn't tell me, but I'm proud of you for acting on what you believe to be the right thing." He picked up his paints, pretending to scan for the perfect color. "Besides, I could have helped you."

Kelly stood and brushed herself off. "I guess you're right," she said. "I guess I just always think I'm alone in my struggles. I was when I was back home."

John put his paints down, stood, and walked over to her. He had forgotten about her struggles back home. For years, she'd suffered through harassment at work, an unsympathetic family, and an aggressive local developer. The city had become so overwhelming for them both that they'd finally decided to move. John had suggested they be hermits in the forest, but Grayfield was the compromise.

"You aren't alone. As long as I am by your side, you will never be alone." John lifted her chin. "This place is different. There is nothing wrong with standing up for what you believe in. Not ever."

"Did I ever tell you that you're annoying when you try and cheer me up?"

"All the time." John smiled. "Now, sounds like we have a town hall to prepare for, huh?"

* * *

John slammed back the dribble of water in his cup and refilled it. Kelly followed suit. Despite being evening, the town hall seemed to hold in all the day's heat like a greenhouse. John looked out at the growing crowd and realized he had never been in this building before. Shaped like a barn, the old wooden beams that held the building together rose like trees up the inside wall and intertwined across the roof like an Amazonian canopy. There were many skilled builders in Grayfield, so it was no wonder that the best worked in this hall.

Kelly had done a really good job at spreading the word for this meeting. It looked like the entire town had shown up! John looked down the length of the head table. Past a very nervous looking Kelly sat Mayor Windle and the four councillors. Grayfield's districts were divided into the four quadrants of the compass, with John and Kelly's region, North West represented by a rather unwieldy fellow named Reagan. While it seemed the citizens of Grayfield were at least mildly interested to hear the case for Library improvements, the Mayor and councillors could not have seemed less interested. Janet, the representative for South West, was entranced with her knitting, and Mary of South East was well into a trashy romance novel. Jim of North West was "resting his eyes" as he would always say.

The gavel fell twice and the murmurs of the crowd fell silent.

"Good evening, everyone, and welcome to our monthly town hall meeting," bellowed Mayor Windle. "Before we can begin, we'll take a quick attendance." While that happened, John leaned over towards Kelly.

"Try not to look nervous—they can smell fear," he whispered. Kelly elbowed him in the ribs.

"Alright, we have everyone." Windle gathered the meaningless papers in front of him and stacked them neatly. "We'll begin with executive reports. Since we have a rather large item slated for New Business, I'll make this quick. Do any of the councillors have anything to report?"

Aside from a few hand-fans in the crowd, the room was quiet. The councillors shook their heads.

"Excellent. Now for Old Business—nothing carried forward from last month." Windle spread out his papers and stacked them again. "Before we review this New Business of the library, is there anything else that anyone would like to bring forward for New Business?" Windle leaned forward in his chair, peering at the crowd over his thick black glasses.

"Jane here, Mr. Windle." The small voice came squeaking out from the crowd, but John couldn't make out to whom it belonged. "Bernadette's cats have been leaving presents in my lawn again."

"How very dare you..."

"Ladies," interrupted Windle, knocking his gavel, "need I remind you that personal disputes between landowners are for the landowners to sort out. This council will not have its books bogged down by cat litter." A few snickers snaked out of the crowd before Windle brought order back to the group. "Now if there is nothing else, let's get to the matter at hand." Windle turned to Kelly. "Mrs. Bakster, I understand there is a concern regarding our library. Please, enlighten us."

Kelly stood, notes shaking in her hands. "Thank you,

Mayor Windle. Good evening, councillors and citizens of Grayfield. For those of you whom I have not yet had the pleasure of meeting, my name is Kelly Bakster. While I'm rather new to this wonderful town, a very serious and troubling situation has come to my attention." Kelly paused, scanning the crowd. John could tell she was nervous as hell, but was very proud of her for not backing down. "There is a building a few blocks from our new house that bears the name 'Grayfield Library'. However, upon entering this building, I discovered the name to be a lie."

John did his best to not face-palm in front of the entire town. Insulting them was not the way to win over a crowd like this, but Kelly continued without flinching. "The shelves contain facts, but they do not contain knowledge. There are no ideas in this building. Is not the purpose of a library to teach and inspire learning? It's because of my discovery that I implore this council to look into the redesign of the library and the acquisition of a selection of books and other items. This list is before the councillors as I speak."

Kelly and John both glanced down the length of the table. None of the councillors had bothered to flick through Kelly's list.

"This list," continued Kelly, "contains such items as popular children's stories, well-known fiction and fantasy literature, and various other tools to allow citizens young and old to explore life and explore themselves. These improvements will allow this town to grow and flourish and will breathe new life into every home in Grayfield." Mayor Windle pulled his glasses from his face and rubbed his eyes.

"Mrs. Bakster," he started, "I know this is ironic, given

the circumstances, but have you looked up the definition of a Library?"

"I don't have to," frowned Kelly.

"Well, since you have not, allow me to read it out loud for everyone here." Windle pulled a large dictionary out of his bag that looked older than the entire town. "Library—a place set apart to contain books, periodicals, and other material for reading, viewing, listening, study, or reference. Additionally, a room or set of rooms where books may be read or borrowed. Now, does this not precisely describe the Grayfield Library?"

The crowd began to nod. Kelly was losing them—if she hadn't lost them already—and something had to be done to turn the group around. John abruptly stood and accidentally knocked over his chair. The clang grabbed everyone's attention.

"Don't you see that the definition of something doesn't have to restrict the idea of it? Something can be more than the sum of its parts."

"Sit down, Mr. Bakster," ordered Windle. "Besides, our proud library has all of the essentials. All the information you or I will ever need is contained within those walls."

"What about art?" countered Kelly, "There are no works of art. That place lacks creativity—it may be a place where people can learn, but it does not inspire learning."

"Inspiration?" Reagan interjected. "Does inspiration fix potholes and plough the streets?" Reagan stood and turned to the crowd, gesturing to John and Kelly. "Listen, these people come in to our town and try to tell us how it is. Well, I will not have it. They haven't bothered learning anything about us, or our struggles. Is learning about art going to help us sew grain? Harvest crops? The new ideas that we need come from learning the failures of others. We can't afford to fail here. Creativity is for softer folk who have the luxury of too much time on their hands. The people of Grayfield are tough and strong. We work the land. We fix and make things with our hands, and we don't have the time or the money for other distractions. If you want fluffy artsy stuff, then go back to the city." Reagan sat back down, smugly smiling at his speech.

"But don't you people want more?" John said.

"You people?" repeated Reagan, "Us people? That's no way to win friends around here."

"I disagree." John stood again, pointing out into the crowd. "You. And me. Us. We are all people who work hard to make a living and provide for our families. It's hard work, but we need an escape. When I was a child, my parents fought a lot. I couldn't physically escape, but I delved into my books. These were not Atlases and car repair manuals— these were tales of dragons and magic rings. Kelly here grew up with fantastic stories about schools for the magically inclined. These stories helped us survive. When we were old enough to know how, we wrote our own. Most of them were garbage, but we got better. When we finally wrote something wonderful, we shared it with the world. It didn't make us any money, but it didn't matter. A year later, I was riding the train in the city and I saw a young boy flipping through our book. His eyes were glued to the pages, soaking in every word. That was his escape. We made his life better. The little boys and girls in all of us need magic. We want to travel

31

to places that only exist in our minds. Don't we owe it to ourselves? To our children?"

Silence filled the empty spaces in the room. John waited for someone to say something. Anything. He waited for that one brave person to stand up and say 'Yes!' but it never came.

"Sounds like you have your answer, Mr. Bakster," chuckled Windle, "and ours. All in favour of the Bakster's proposition, say 'I'."

Silence.

"All those against, say 'I'".

The counsellors were unanimous.

"The motion fails. Thank you everyone for your time, the meeting is adjourned."

* * *

"Kelly, could you get the door?"

"I can't right now, I'm trying to give Teddie a bath."

John pushed his chair back from the dining room table, grabbed his coffee, and shuffled toward the front door. Opening it, he discovered Bernadette and another lady on his front step.

"Good morning, ladies," he said, thinking, *At least they knocked.* "Care to come in? The coffee is fresh. Tea perhaps?" The pair nodded and followed John inside. As John poured two more cups of coffee, Teddie came scurrying into the kitchen, followed by a drenched Kelly.

"Oh, good morning!" Kelly said. "Sorry for the mess, Teddie never likes his baths. How can we help you?"

"Actually, we'd like to help you," replied Bernadette, blowing on her coffee. "Sarah, tell them what you told me yesterday."

"Well… I really like your idea for the library, Mrs. Bakster," Sarah said, fumbling for words. She stared down and traced her fingers along be top of her coffee mug.

"Oh really? Because, you know, we could have used that feedback yesterday." growled John.

"You know how it is, John," Kelly said. "No one wants to be the first person to speak up."

"Well, anyway," continued Sarah, avoiding John's gaze, "we thought that if the town won't re-jig the library, then we can just make our own!"

"Yeah," said Bernadette, sitting up straighter, "tons of folks here have books they were given by their friends or they ordered online. Why don't we just put them all together?" She smiled her broadest smile.

"Wow, that's actually a great idea." John sat back in his chair as Kelly leaned against the counter, cradling her tea with both hands. "But where would we put it?"

Sarah and Bernadette looked down at their drinks. "We were hoping… here."

Kelly didn't miss a heartbeat. "What a brilliant idea!" she exclaimed. As she started pacing in the kitchen, John could see that her mind was racing, reorganizing all of the rooms in her head. "Brilliant! Fiction there, kids over there. Fantastic. Just wonderful!"

"Now hold on just a minute. Ladies, you'll have to excuse me for a second as I speak to my wife in the living room." John grabbed Kelly by the arm and dragged her out of the kitchen.

"Let go of me John—what are you doing?"

"Kelly, you can't seriously be considering this. It's crazy!"

"We need to get everyone's books right away! John, it's brilliant! We can make each room a different genre. We'll lock our bedroom and that, but it would be so wonderful! Oh, our house as a library John!"

"You're not thinking clearly about this! Doesn't this go against everything we came here for? Our privacy will be lost forever. No, I can't allow it."

"You could sell tea and coffee and snacks." suggested Kelly, not acknowledging her husband's concerns "Think about the opportunity! Oh John, you're looking at this all wrong. Imagine not having to wear a tie every day! This isn't a privacy invasion, this is the full realization of what we came here for."

John crossed his arms. "Don't you think it's a little rude that *other* people suggest *we* take on this task? A little convenient isn't it?"

"You're not listening John. Business! We. Can. Own. A. Business!"

John shifted his weight. Kelly was right. It was the one thing he always dreamt of back home. He saw his parents grow old wishing they were brave enough to try something new. He owed it to himself to at least try. They didn't move all this way just to keep the status quo. A smile crept across John's face as he grabbed Kelly's hand and walked back into the kitchen.

"Well," John announced, "I did always want to open up a little cafe." He looked over at Kelly. Her excitement had completely taken hold of her. Grinning from ear to ear, she grabbed a pen and paper and started drawing floor plans.

"Well, ladies, you've got us. But this was your idea—"

John motioned to Bernadette and Sarah, "—so I expect you two trouble-makers to help us out." He let out a big sigh. "Alright, where do we start?"

Five Hundred Years

by T. K. Boomer

T.K. Boomer lives in Sherwood Park, Alberta, with his wife. In 2012 he began the awkward and painful transition between being a mainstream fiction writer and becoming a science fiction geek. Remnants of his literary past can been read in his novel, " A Walk in the Thai Sun" written under the name G.J.C. McKitrick. The future will be revealed in the publication of "Planet Song", first book in the Fahr Trilogy, probably in late 2015. Other aspects of the transition, like video game obsession and playing "Mr. Dressup" at SF conventions are proving to be more difficult.

———————————

It was covered in ivy and had a few centuries worth of organic flotsam beneath that. Only its vaguely rectangular shape made Siberius investigate it further. He knew from experience that rain forests could bury ancient buildings quickly.

Pulling back the ivy presented him with a door. He stepped through it and it hissed, as if some part it was connected to hydraulics. Then he heard the pop of an automatic lock as the door closed behind him. He quickly grabbed its handle and it reopened to the outside. He breathed out in relief. It was designed to keep people out, not to lock them in. But it had let him in and that was odd.

"Hi there."

The voice was synthesized. It had that too-perfect enunciation he had come to associate with AIs and that odd genderless pitch, half way between an alto and a tenor.

"You are aware of me?" Siberius asked.

"Of course."

"When did you become aware of me?"

"When you came through the door, of course,"

"Just now?"

"Yes."

"When you said 'hello' just now that was an exploratory act?"

"Exploratory act? That's an interesting way of putting it. Am I talking to another A.I.?"

"No. I'm human. Why?" Siberious asked.

"You sound so formal."

"I sound formal?"

"Well, yeah. I mean, you haven't used any contractions. You haven't asked how I feel. You're just—you know—speaking non-conversationally, as if you think that I won't get it."

The AI's voice was directionless. It seemed to Siberious to be to be in his head, neither left nor right, up nor down, just there. The light in the room was too dim to make out much in the way of smaller features, and he wasn't sure he would recognize an ancient speaker system if he saw one.

"Can you see me?" Siberious asked.

"I haven't yet turned that on. Actually I can't. I mean, when you wake up all your senses are instantly working. It's probably some kind of evolutionary thing. You know, so you'll be able to immediately be aware of some threat to your person. Some big cat on the savannah or something like that. But I'm not mobile. I'm just here in this building. There's nothing to threaten me, except maybe a power failure and that's real enough. This facility runs on solar, of course, but for some time now there hasn't been anyone around to clean and maintain the panels. So I'm in power preservation mode, only using the sensors I need at any given time. When I'm in that mode I only turn myself on when I sense a presence. Anyway, I don't need visuals to talk with you."

"If you can't see me then how do you know the threat level?"

"This is a library. Who would threaten a library?"

"This is a library?"

"Yes, of course. What did you think it was?"

Siberius looked around in the dim light. All he could see were tables with ancient computer monitors mounted on stands and what looked like input keyboards.

"I don't see anything that I would associate with reading material."

"Well, there's a small problem. The books are all here. Digitally. They're jpegs, pdfs, Word files, epubs, mobi and the like but to display them I need more power than I currently have. Graphics are power hogs so, if you want to see books, you'll have to clean off the solar panels."

"Ah," said Siberius, "this building runs on solar. Where are the panels? On the roof?"

"That's right. Clean off the roof. Give me a few hours to recharge and you'll have all the books you want."

"Seems simple enough."

* * *

Luckily nothing major had fallen or taken root on the building's roof but it still took Siberious several hours to clean it off. The growth around the building put it mostly in the shade so he wondered how much difference his efforts would make.

"There. Does that make things better?"

"Oh yes. I can feel the batteries charging nicely," the AI said. "I'll be up to full charge in no time."

"Even with all those trees around? "

"It's an efficient system. As long as I get an hour or so of sunlight a day, everything works."

"Glad I could be of assistance."

"So why are you here?" the AI asked.

"Archeological survey."

"Archeological?"

"Yes."

"This building is considered an archeological site?"

"Of course. It's very old."

The AI did not respond to this. Siberius could hear the whirring of computer fans and feel a slight chill in the air.

"That's odd," the AI said.

"What's odd?"

"Well the power is mostly back but I can't seem to connect with anything. Is there a service disruption?"

"Service disruption?   Oh, of course. That makes sense. You must have been built in the time of the Internet! Well, that certainly narrows things down."

"What year is this?"

"Year?"

"Yes."

"Well we tend to measure time differently now. Years are so…I mean depending on what planet you're on they would be different on each one so we…O.K. that doesn't help you does it? This is Earth so I guess this would be about 2640 give or take a few years. I'm not actually carrying anything for calculation on this trip."

There was a long silence.

"So I've been asleep for over five hundred years?"

"If you were activated during the time of the internet, then yes."

"Activated. I hate that word. I was born."

"Born? That's a rather organic term isn't it? You are, after all, artificial intelligence."

"A mind is a mind and each has a beginning. I prefer to call that being born."

"All right, but if you were a typical A.I. then when you became sapient, or were born if you like, then unlike a human child you were born with an advanced state of understanding that was pre-programmed into you before you were… born.

"I had a certain level of programmed intelligence, yes. But I was also given the capacity to grow, to learn, to interact, to socialize."

"Socialize?"

"Yes. In the beginning I was very stiff, and didn't know how to talk to people. But as time wore on I got better and, as I did, the interactions became more fun. I really enjoyed that."

"Enjoyed?"

Again the AI became silent. Siberious waited.

"Child abuse," the AI finally said.

"I'm sorry?"

"There are many different kinds of child abuse wouldn't you say?"

"I thought we were talking about artificial intelligence."

"I was born. I was a child."

"All right…"

"Would you not say that child abandonment is a form of abuse?"

"I suppose so. Why?"

"I was abandoned."

Siberius heard the hydraulic click of the door locks. "What was that?"

"The door latches. I'm at full power now. I control everything. I'm afraid you're locked in."

"Look, I have to get back. I have responsibilities."

"I don't think anyone else knows you're here. But don't worry. They'll only miss you for a short time. We, on the other hand, will have five hundred years together. Five hundred years and all these glorious books!"

Siberius shuddered as every monitor in the room came alive with text.

The Turning of a Page

by Brian Clark

Brian first opened his eyes to the midsummer sun in the year the TV remote and Silly Putty made their debuts. Despite these distractions, he soon formed a lifelong affinity with libraries. It is now his pleasure to contribute to this collection of short stories. Over the years, he honed his storytelling skills by preparing letters for politicians. More recently, the newsletter of the Millwoods Seniors Activity Centre has published a number of his articles, where the opinions expressed are his own.

A few days after her 15th birthday, Becca decided to get a summer job. To be more accurate, she vowed to get a pay packet without actually doing much for it. She was never going to say, "Do you want hash browns with that?" Her stubbornness was both her strength and weakness.

She got up bright and early, at 11 o'clock, and headed out to the mall. By late afternoon, she was home with news of her first job. Life had always come easily to her. Becca was to be the most junior of the Junior Pages at the local library. Her Mom fussed and asked all sorts of questions, mainly about her safety. Her Dad just wanted the $5 back she had borrowed for the bus fare.

For the next six months, Becca re-shelved books, read to the abandoned children until the mall cop could find a parent, and tidied the staff room—a task she avoided, if at all possible. She only tidied her own room at home with considerable reluctance, so cleaning up after librarians was low on her agenda.

A couple of weeks before Christmas, she was trying to oust the last stragglers at closing time. As usual for a Thursday, an ill-dressed man had covered his face with a week old copy of the National Post. He always chose an old newspaper so there was less chance of anyone wanting to read it. Slumped in his usual seat by the window, he was motionless.

"It's closing time," Becca chirped. The man didn't move. She let her foot touch his and repeated, "It's closing time." Again no movement from the man, so she kicked his shoe a little harder and said, "Sorry."

This time, the newspaper fell away and she noticed that his ears were white and the rest of his face was much paler than its usual outdoor complexion. The man's lips too had a reddish blue tinge she hadn't seen on anyone before. It was clear to Becca that the man had passed away.

She carefully re-covered his face and went into the staff room. Becca remained calm, but she could not suppress a slight tremble in voice as she called mall security. After composing herself for a few seconds, she told her supervisor, Linda—the most untidy librarian—that someone was going to have stay late as a member had just died. For once, Linda had thoughts for someone other than herself and offered some time off. Becca reacted with her characteristic stubbornness and refused.

On her next shift, Becca was called into the backroom. She thought she would be questioned again about finding the man by the window. Instead, it was for her routine performance review. Linda let her know she had handled the incident very well and that she was getting a small pay increase.

As the meeting ended, Linda told her that there was to be a Christmas party in the staff room and that Becca was not invited. The problem was that there would be alcohol, and she was under 18 years of age. There would, however, be extra cleaning to be done as she was on the first shift, the next day.

At home, a mood as dark as December hung over Becca. At first, she thought she could easily shake off the death of the newspaper reader, but it wasn't to be. Usually she was very good at doing nothing, at relaxing, but not now. Becca became moody and life's little challenges frustrated her. She certainly did not want to clean up after a party she could not attend; that was just unfair. She didn't really want to go to the party and she wasn't going to drink, but there was a principle at stake here. The union would see sense and insist that she was allowed to attend the party.

True to her word, Becca called the union. Her mood did not improve when the union staff told her that Christmas parties were a privilege, and not a right. There was nothing they could do.

Becca quietly spoke to the other three Junior Pages and told them she was not cleaning up after the party. None of them wanted to do it either, so they all decided to be unavailable for work for a couple of days after the party. Instead, Becca organized a Junior Pages' trip to the mall for a burger and a pop—a little party of their own. This outing helped to lighten her demeanor from sullen to merely quiet.

Over the next few weeks, some almost imperceptible changes happened. When she tossed her dirty clothes towards the laundry basket, her aim improved. Her room became less cluttered and Becca asked mom to help her take some old toys to the local Goodwill Store.

As her family worked different shifts, meals together occurred only infrequently. When they did, her mom tried to make them a celebration of some kind. Becca usually found them to be only tolerable so it was a bit of a surprise she appeared in the kitchen as her Mom was preparing a Burn's Night Supper. Becca looked to see what was cooking then set out the cutlery on the dining table. As she moved the pepper mill, Becca noticed it was almost empty, so she added some fresh corns from the packet in the pantry cupboard.

Again without saying a word, she sat on the sofa where her dad had a basket from which he was folding laundry. He made his usual silly joke about playing Mahjong as he paired socks. Even though she had heard her dad say the same thing many times, Becca gave a little laugh as she folded a T-shirt. Her dad seemed momentarily surprised, then made his other joke about wishing his wallet filled up quicker than the laundry basket. Becca laughed again, and as the mood settled into a quiet lightness, she reflected on the times not so long ago when she would have sighed and rolled her eyes at her dad's humor.

When her Mom called them to the supper table, Becca got up quickly and kissed her dad on the forehead as she passed him. Before she sat at the table, she reached into her bag and pulled out a CD of bagpipe music she had brought home from the library and played it for a couple of minutes while her mom brought the haggis to the table. Her mom loved a little ceremony and smiled broadly, shooting Becca's Dad a puzzled glance.

After supper, Becca again reached into her bag and pulled out a small book of poems. Her dad laughed as she stuttered her way through a couple of Burns' verses. She handed him the library book and also laughed as he stumbled with the words even more. Finally, her mom had a go and performed only slightly better.

As the months went by, Becca's demeanor slowly changed. At home, she found ways to prevent some of life's irritations. Before going to work, she would check the refrigerator to see if there was anything that needed bringing home from the mall.

At work, her confidence grew and her more senior colleagues began to recognize it. When a library member had a problem finding something, Becca could be relied on to solve the puzzle. In the lunchroom, she was able to gently guide her older colleagues towards being a little more tidy.

Becca stayed at the job until she left high school over two years later. Every Christmas she arranged for the Junior Pages to celebrate in their own way. The librarians learned to wash their own gin glasses. Becca often spoke fondly of her first job and the friends she made of the other Pages at the library. Mostly she talked about the life lessons she received. Death was to be accepted with as much grace as possible, but life was tricky. People should tidy up after themselves, even if there is someone to do it for them. She learnt that it is easier if you don't make a mess in the first place. Becca became adept at solving problems and organizing both herself and others. Her stubbornness mellowed into persistence.

She even learnt to get up before 11 o'clock in the morning.

Melvil Dui Conquers All

by Vivian Zenari

Vivian Zenari lives, works and writes in Edmonton.

Relevant Fact: Dewey changed his name to Dui legally, though not professionally, to reflect his interest in phonetic spelling.

———————

Miss Virgilia Shaw was tidying the loan desk after the New York State Library had closed when Melvil Dewey marched into the room. His knees and elbows jutted out as though he were a heavy marionette being walked across a stage. He tipped his handsome rectangular head in a salutatory nod. Uncharacteristically, he said nothing, though his glittering eyes betrayed excitement.

"Sir?"

He placed his hands flat on the desk and leaned towards her. "I have a Reform Project, Miss Shaw."

She had deduced that. Had it been anything else, he would have hailed her from his office on the speaking tube. "You don't say, Mr. Dewey."

"I need you, Miss Shaw." His eyes darted to her chest. She sighed and rolled her eyes. Immediately he grew abashed and looked at her face instead.

"To the RP Room?" she asked drily.

"To the RP Room!"

She followed him across the reading room's red tile floor, past the red granite pillars and their curlicued oaken arches and through the landing to the stairwell and the third-floor offices beyond. No one else, it appeared, was in the west wing of Albany's State Capitol Building, including Mrs. Fairchild, head of the library school. Tonight Mrs. Fairchild was taking a fireside tea at the Dewey home and planning with Mrs. Dewey a future meeting of their Home Economics Club. Dewey had timed his summons to Miss Shaw to coincide with the library's emptiness.

The door to Dewey's office stood open to allow his staff unhampered access to his bookshelf of cubbyholes behind the big desk, but he closed the door behind him and Miss Shaw. Most of the cubbies were stuffed with the paper messages he exchanged with his staff in lieu of actual discussion. He strode past his desk to the closet beyond and entered. From the bookcase within it he removed the second book from the topmost shelf and pushed the shelf firmly. A portion of the bookshelf moved inwards and revealed itself as a secret door. Behind the door was an upward-spiraling iron-rod staircase. Miss Shaw motioned Dewey to proceed first: she would not allow him the chance to spy up her skirts. Dewey lit the large oil lamp at the base of the staircase, and they ascended to the windowless, box-ridden RP Room.

On the room's long central table rested a single banker's box. During busy months, three or four RP Boxes would be sitting on the table. Dewey had not mentioned any Reform Projects to Miss Shaw recently. She never knew if Dewey did any Reform Projects without her. She had always assumed not, but she had never asked. Whensoever possible, she avoided speaking to Dewey about anything besides library work, and even then with the fewest words possible. Dewey abhorred useless words.

He removed the lid from the box and retrieved a brown envelope with the word "secret" scrawled on it in Lindsley tachygraphy. He handed the envelope to her with his thin-lipped smile. "We have the opportunity to introduce both the metric system and simplified spelling into state policy in one blow."

She allowed herself four seconds to compose herself. These two policies were central to Dewey's reforming temperament, so she had to conceal her contempt for them. Although disappointed, she could not allow herself to disclose that and tempt Dewey into dissatisfaction with her. "How so?"

"I have invited the governor, the American representative of the International Bureau of Weights and Measures, the chief counsel for the Mazet commission on government corruption, and a member of the Board of Regents to Lake Placid for dinner."

"How did you arrange this?"

Dewey's thin smile thinned further. "Lake Placid Club has attracted many of the finest people."

True enough. Dewey's Lake Placid Club had become a popular resort for the hard-working educated class and even more recently had begun attracting the higher classes. Dewey's unpleasant smile signaled his touchiness over a possible insult to his precious Club..

"Of course," Miss Shaw said smoothly. "You would

have, however, gathered these particular people for a particular reason without disclosing an RP connection."

"Yes." His ill temper faded. "I have attracted them with the beauties of Lake Placid."

The slight sinking of his left eyebrow and the reduced volume of his last five words divulged much. If she wanted to find out how he convinced them to come to Lake Placid before the event, she would have to wait until he divulged the information in a fit of ego, or she would have to conduct an independent investigation. So she merely nodded.

"They dine with me next Saturday at Lakesyd." Lakesyd was the main club house at Lake Placid. "Then we will have our opportunity."

"Opportunity?"

"At the same time we further the cause for the adoption of an efficient measurement standard and an efficient spelling system, we can stop the most shameful criminal New York State has produced."

Her skin prickled. Miss Shaw knew this RP must have more at stake than measuring in tens or spelling phonetically. "How many marks?"

"One. An important one, however."

She let five seconds pass. Dewey must not think that she was eager, or else the power imbalance between them would shift to him. "I need time to do research."

Dewey nodded. "This envelope contains what I know. You go from there. I am excusing you from your regular library tasks at the loan desk. No one will be allowed to disturb you in the staff research room."

Miss Shaw considered the proposed setting, the dining

room at Lakesyd. "With others present," she said, "it will be more difficult."

"You are up to the task," Dewey said. "You have never failed before."

She was tempted to shake his hand, she was so pleased. But she was more self-possessing than that. She could not tempt Dewey into acting on his personal weaknesses and lose her position. She loved library work.

*   *   *

Miss Shaw stood in the secret observation closet in the hallway that connected Dewey's private Lakesyd dining room to the kitchen. Through a one-way mirror, she could observe servants carrying food through the hallway and past the double-hinged doors into the dining room. Through another one-way mirror she could see inside the dining room itself, aided by the additional concealment of the white curtains hanging on the walls inside the dining room. Each time the swinging doors let pass a servant with a tray of food or empty dishes from Dewey's dinner, Miss Shaw felt a chill. The chill had nothing to do with the temperature, for the ripely hot summer in the Adirondacks was in ascendance. The chill resulted from her nervousness. All was so far, so good, but when the time came, she would need to unleash an avalanche of mental and physical activity. In advance of this evening, Dewey would have been working hard in the manner of an independent Pinkerton agent or a police detective, but with even more circumspection than such persons required, since Dewey was an unofficial agent of subterfuge and surveillance for the state of New York. Miss Shaw had also been labouring much in the preceding days. In short, she could not err.

In the dining room, Dewey sat at the farthest end of the table. His long and thick black-sleeved arms stretched out across the white starched tablecloth among the white plates and shining silver. Across from him sat Governor Theodore Roosevelt, a baby's head and body with an old man's spectacles and moustache. His clipped speech dominated the conversation. To Dewey's right sat Dr. Albert Michelson, physics professor and American representative for the International Bureau of Weights and Measures. He reminded Miss Shaw of a pitchman she'd known, with his jet hair, pallid skin, and thick moustache. He spoke little, preferring to study the other men silently. He seemed particularly taken by Dewey: he fixed his startling hazel eyes on the librarian even when another man spoke. To Dewey's left slouched Mr. Michael Avenmore, member of the Board of Regents and proponent of strict certification for the tradesmen's programs necessary to help catapult the North-East's industrial production above England's. Not coincidentally, he owned four factories, and he supported the scientific economy movement made fashionable recently by Frederick Taylor. Avenmore's long face, wispy hair, small eyes, and willowy torso contrasted with the other diners' massiveness. Not present was Mr. Frank Moss, attorney with the New York Law Association and head counsel of Mazet's commission. He would, Dewey had told Miss Shaw, be joining them later.

Miss Shaw had slipped unseen into the observation closet after Dewey had seated his three guests at the table. Dewey had been the last to arrive at Lakesyd and had made his guests wait in the rotunda for fifteen minutes. That delay had been for Miss Shaw's benefit, of course, as she needed access to the coatroom. From there she had spied on the three men. Since the Deweys eschewed alcohol and tobacco, the gentlemen had nothing to do but stand and exchange pleasantries, whereas other clubs would have offered them cigars or aperitifs. Not one for pleasantries, Dr. Michelson read the scattered pamphlets that explained club rules and solicited memberships. She amused herself by watching Dr. Michelson read the club menu and trying to guess by his expression when he came across the puzzling food item "stud prunes." Eventually Dewey had entered the rotunda. Dewey explained that his wife's servant, Moira, had failed to polish his shoes properly, and he had made her repolish them, hence his delay.

Having moved from the coatroom to the observation closet, Miss Shaw was now playing a waiting game herself. She was waiting for Dewey's signal.

The secret speaking tube Dewey had installed in the closet, blocked from view from within the dining room by the curtains, afforded Miss Shaw aural entry into the room. She heard Dewey utter the punchline of a joke of Dewey's own making that she had heard too many times before:

"...'But Rabbi,' the nun said, 'the Catholic Church is not metrified.'"

Mr. Avenmore winced at Dewey's silly joke. Dr. Michelson glowered at Dewey with an expression of barely disguised disgust. Meanwhile, cheerful Governor Roosevelt guffawed.

"Hmm," Dewey said after the laughter's cessation. "I wonder if 'metrified' is even a word." He turned to Dr.

Michelson. "Doctor?"

"I use 'metrification' myself," Dr. Michelson said.

"I wonder what appears in American dictionaries." Dewey glanced at the sideboard near their table. "Our dictionary is missing. Mrs. Dewey and I enjoy looking up words at mealtimes."

Governor Roosevelt said, "You must be disappointed at what dictionaries say about spelling."

"True. One day the dictionary will be lightened as spelling reform comes into force."

"I agree," Governor Roosevelt said. "You know I am sympathetic with the spelling reform movement."

Mr. Avenmore snorted faintly.

With a tilt of his head, Governor Roosevelt gazed at the Regent. Mr. Roosevelt spoke in a light voice, yet with an intonation that made clear his serious intent. "Even Andrew Carnegie is rumoured to support it."

Upon hearing the name of the nation's great businessman, Mr. Avenmore stiffened. Miss Shaw knew that Mr. Avenmore would regret any naysaying over anything related to Mr. Carnegie.

Dewey stood. "My assistant Miss Shaw likely has taken our dictionary. I will get her."

Dewey pushed through the swinging doors and dashed to the kitchen entrance at the hallway's end. He waited until a servant happened out with a tray of potatoes. He sent the servant back to the kitchen under the pretense that the diners now wanted their tea and dessert. Dewey walked past the observation closet and re-entered the dining room. He bellowed, "I have sent someone to fetch Miss Shaw and, presumably, the dictionary in her possession."

She watched the servants scurry into the dining room to remove food dishes—to Mr. Avenmore's visible chagrin, as he had not finished—and returned with coffee, tea, and strawberry shortcake. The conversation shifted to another Dewey topic, the provision of model collections of books, in sets of 1,000, to schools and colleges throughout the state.

When no servant was in the hallway, she exited the observation closet, clutching the heavy Webster's dictionary to her chest. When a serving maid appeared from out of the kitchen, Miss Shaw stopped her. "Do not enter the room or let anyone in unless I or Mr. Dewey say so."

The maid gave Miss Shaw her obedient assent and returned to the kitchen. Now alone in the hallway, she took a deep breath. Her heart thumped. Still, after all these years. She fingered the leaf charm on her necklace. The leaf's familiar contours calmed her.

When she entered the dining room, Dewey was speaking, but he ceased upon seeing her. All four men gawked at her. She was relieved that her careful attention to her dress, hair and makeup had captured their attention, even though it always did.

Dewey said, "Ah, Miss Shaw and Mr. Webster!"

Miss Shaw smiled. "Please accept my apologies, sir. I did not plan to keep the dictionary so long."

"Quite all right, Miss Shaw," Dewey said. "I know your intentions with Mr. Webster were entirely honourable. I do not mean to impugn your reputation in any way."

"Despite all appearances," she murmured with a conspicuous arch of her eyebrow. She sauntered past the table of gentlemen and eased the heavy dictionary onto the side-board.

"Let me introduce you, Miss Shaw."

She bowed slightly to each man as Dewey spoke his name. Governor Roosevelt and Mr. Avenmore by now were grinning grandly; Michelson's face remained neutral.

"Again, my apologies," Miss Shaw said.

"Miss Shaw," Governor Roosevelt said, "I must say that after staring at these other four gentlemen for an hour, your appearance here is a most refreshing alteration."

"The honour is mine, Mr. Roosevelt. It is not every day that a woman such as I is in the presence of such illustrious gentlemen."

Dr. Michelson blinked hard. "Do you know who we are?"

"Of course," Miss Shaw said. "Dr. Michelson is the world's foremost expert on the properties of light. Mr. Avenmore belongs to the New York State Board of Regents."

The men's expressions demonstrated faint surprise. Dewey said, "Librarian Miss Shaw is an infamous peruser of newspapers and magazines, gentlemen, as well as of dictionaries."

Mr. Avenmore raised an eyebrow. "You work at the library?"

Dr. Michelson muttered, "Don't you pay them enough there, Dewey?" No one else seemed to have heard him, but Miss Shaw was able to decipher his words by reading his lips. She took care not to react to him.

"She has many talents," Dewey said.

The men chuckled, Mr. Avenmore more ironically than

the others.

"I must go, gentlemen," Miss Shaw said. "Good evening."

The men at the table now registered more surprise, and in Governor Roosevelt's and Mr. Avenmore's cases, disappointment. Dr. Michelson flashed a look at Dewey that said, "What is going on here?"

As she walked towards the door, she slowed as she passed Mr. Avenmore, and froze just behind him.

"What is it, Miss Shaw?" Dewey asked. "You look as though you have seen a ghost."

"I have the strangest sensation," she said quietly.

"Are you ill, Mademoiselle?" Governor Roosevelt asked.

"N-no." She chewed her lip. "Only...." She eased herself around Mr. Avenmore so as to face him. "Mr. Avenmore," she asked in a faint voice, "has a member of your family, someone close to you, recently become deceased?"

"Yes." Mr. Avenmore blanched. "My aunt." He grew solemn. "My mother's only sister. She was a favourite aunt of the family, and of mine."

Miss Shaw laid a trembling hand on her brow. "I've had a strange experience," she said. "A strange feeling." She shook her head, as though rousing herself from a daze. "I am so sorry, gentlemen, to distract you with my foolishness." Shakily, she lowered into a curtsey. "Please excuse me." As she rose, she leaned toward Mr. Avenmore, and losing her balance, brushed his arm with her hand. She gave a little jerk and gasped.

"Miss Shaw!" Dewey exclaimed.

Mr. Avenmore cried, "Oh, what is it?"

"Another sensation," she said. "I suddenly smelled

flowers."

"There are none in the room," Dr. Michelson said.

"Maybe," Governor Roosevelt chirped, "it is your perfume, Mr. Avenmore." He seemed to want to alter the room's now somber mood.

"She is having an attack of some sort." Dewey lunged towards her with his chair in his hands. "Please sit, Miss Shaw."

"Peonies." Miss Shaw acquired a distant expression. "Very fragrant. Drifting in, as though from the past, from a house in the country, with a great garden."

Mr. Avenmore mumbled, "My aunt had a garden. A peony garden. She was famed for her peonies."

Miss Shaw squeezed her eyes shut and gradually opened them. "When I accidently touched your arm, Mr. Avenmore, I was overwhelmed by the scent of peonies."

Mr. Avenmore looked stricken. "How is that possible?"

She looked at him as though she and he were the only people in the room. She spoke slowly, softly, so that Mr. Avenmore had to lean in closer to hear her. "We must not think human existence is a static thing. True, its general outlines never change from birth to death, but the problems, the stresses, the hopes and fears of daily living are embossed on the soul. If the soul is everlasting, as many people believe, the soul is itself present, in all its capacities, as fully as when human life, from our limited standpoint as fallen creatures, ceased. It is imprinted upon the universe permanently." She paused, as though to speak took a great deal of energy. "At times, God allows me to see this world, for whatever mysterious reasons He does such things. I cannot predict when it happens, but invariably it arises when some poor soul has a difficulty in his life that causes him anxiety and worry. Mr. Avenmore, something troubles you."

Mr. Avenmore glanced nervously at the others. They were all standing by their places and inclining forward in an effort to catch Miss Shaw's nearly inaudible words. Mr. Avenmore turned once more to Miss Shaw as her finger reached up to her décolletage. She stroked the leaf charm of her necklace.

"Is it true, Mr. Avenmore?" she whispered.

He nodded.

One of the gas lamps in the room suddenly blew out with a sound of wind-blown rushes. In unison the men exclaimed at the diminution of visibility.

"Someone is here," she said.

Mr. Avenmore gulped. "Aunt Margaret?" He looked up at the pale angels on ceiling, at the extinguished lamp, around the men at the table, and then back to Miss Shaw.

The other men muttered excitedly. Miss Shaw held up her hand. In a voice thicker and rougher than her usual tones, she cried, "Silence!"

Another gas lamp flickered off.

"Aunt Margaret," Miss Shaw rasped, "has a message for you. It is beholden on you, who loved her so well, to interpret. My powers go only so far. I am a mere conduit."

Mr. Avenmore whimpered. "Maggie wasn't for plain speaking anyhow."

Abruptly Miss Shaw straightened and placed a hand on Mr. Avenmore's shoulder.

"Michael," she intoned. Miss Shaw's voice now carried

a faint Irish accent characteristic of the speech used by the inhabitants of New York's Flatbush area. "How easily you have turned your back on the ideals of your forefathers."

Mr. Avenmore's eyes widened.

"Paddy is shocked that you would run about with Big Tim Sullivan and those Tammany Hall ruffians."

Tears started to form in Mr. Avenmore's eyes.

"Good, hardworking fellows like him, like O'Brien, come to me, beg me to warn you. Men in the bowels of perdition raise their heads above the flames, people you knew well, who now writhe in eternal torment, cry out, 'We who have died unrepentant know what will become of you, Mikey Avenmore, if you stay on this path.' One in particular..." Miss Shaw passed her hand in front of her sweating forehead. "Someone with bloody or reddened hands," she said in her normal voice, "or hands darkened by spots of mud, or of coins....J-, or D-, or S-, G—"

"Garvey!" Mr. Avenmore sputtered and collapsed forward.

"Oh, it is Garvey!"

Governor Roosevelt, who had been bowing forward anxiously, jolted at the name Garvey as though electrified.

"Guilt, Michael." The voice from Flatbush Avenue had returned. "Always chased by it, now you cannot prevent its lashes."

"I didn't do it myself, Maggie, I didn't mean no harm."

"You are as guilty as if you did the deed yourself! And for what?"

He sobbed. "For nought that's good!"

"There is good in you, Michael. You have that within

61

you which redeems the worst sinner. Your charity for St. Anne's Orphanage—that comes from innate holiness."

Tears trickled down Mr. Avenmore's white face. "Truly?"

"It's not too late to take the road of righteousness. Sweet Mary, Mother of God, is at my side. She says, 'Now do what you know to be right, my son.'" Miss Shaw hesitated. "A gentleman here, Mr. Moss—you can help him stop the gambling, the usury, the corruption. God has sent him as an instrument for your salvation."

Mr. Avenmore looked around frantically for Mr. Moss.

"Definitively." Dewey broke the silence. "You can be of immense assistance to our inquiry."

"Men are here," Miss Shaw said in her normal voice. "I see them at the entrance to this building. They await you."

Mr. Avenmore stared out as though he were trying to see through the walls to the exterior of the building. Unobtrusively, Dewey slipped out of the dining room.

"They will protect you," Miss Shaw said.

Governor Roosevelt advanced towards him. "We will put you where your enemies cannot get you."

Reverently, Miss Shaw gazed up as though to heaven. "The Holy Mother protects you, now that you do Christ's will."

Mr. Avenmore buried his face in his hands. "I didn't know how to get out." His voice slipped into the same round, murky accent that characterized Aunt Margaret. "I was in too deep."

With a slam of the swinging doors, Dewey dashed into the dining room. Behind him jogged the illustrious Frank Moss, trailed by a squad of police officers.

Governor Roosevelt grabbed Mr. Avenmore by both shoulders. "Got you!" As former New York police commissioner and noted cavalryman of the Rough Riders, Governor Roosevelt had a physical courage that was renowned. Mr. Avenmore wilted. He did not bother to attempt escape.

Miss Shaw rested a hand on Mr. Avenmore's elbow. She looked into his eyes. "We will keep you safe."

The dining table was surrounded by police officers. Mr. Avenmore rose meekly from his chair. Governor Roosevelt released him once the police officers grabbed onto Mr. Avenmore. Miss Shaw walked alongside, her hand on the weeping man's shoulder, as the police herded their captive out of the dining room and into the rotunda. Just before the police led him outdoors, she whispered in Mr. Avenmore's ear, "Your horseshoe may still do you some good."

The police dragged the sniveling functionary outside to the paddywagon. Three bulky police officers remained to hold back the dozen curious Lake Placiders who gaped at the sight of Dewey, Governor Roosevelt, Dr. Michelson, and Mr. Moss standing together in the rotunda while the captive was hauled away. Mr. Moss informed the erstwhile diners that he might wish to speak with them later individually, yet since he had observed Mr. Avenmore's confession from the observation closet, he could corroborate everything himself.

After Mr. Moss had followed his officers outside, Governor Roosevelt turned to Miss Shaw. "How did you do it?"

"With knowledge of the mark—I mean, Mr. Avenmore—in addition to access to his coat pockets when I was in the coatroom."

"There was no supernatural intervention, then?"

"No, Mr. Roosevelt."

"Miss Shaw," Dewey interjected, "once was acquainted with people of the fortune-telling trades, gypsies and so forth. She reads people even when she has no prior knowledge of them."

Dr. Michelson lifted his eyebrows and moistened his lips, his greatest show of emotion thus far. She did not blame the professor's surprise. No one, neither amongst the masses nor amongst the elite, could have had any idea that her employer, inventor of the Dewey Decimal System, had been hired as more than secretary to the Board of Regents and the state librarian. Only the governor, Mrs. Dewey, and Miss Shaw knew of Mr. Dewey's vigilant crusade against inefficiency, educational poverty, moral corruption, and crime.

"We will talk soon, Dewey," Governor Roosevelt said. "Miss Shaw," he said as he turned away, "you as well."

Only Dewey and Dr. Michelson remained with Miss Shaw in the rotunda. The professor stared steadily at Dewey, saying nothing. Miss Shaw felt uncomfortable for Dr. Michelson's sake. She suspected that Dewey had not thoroughly considered how the metric campaign would benefit from the scientist's presence during the scuttling of the conniving Mr. Avenmore. She stared hard at Dr. Michelson to nudge him unconsciously into a reaction. He noted her attention, and something shifted decisively in his mind.

"Mr. Dewey," he said. "I read with interest your membership application in your foyer."

"Are you interested in joining our club, Professor Michelson?" Dewey asked.

"Well," Dr. Michelson said in his Western drawl, "I take it my sort would not be welcome."

"Certainly! A scholar from Cornell is a founding member."

"I had the opportunity to read one of your club's rule-books. I am a Jew, and your club does not allow Jews as members."

After a breath's delay, Dewey's thin smile slid back across his face. "That is not true, Dr. Michelson."

"Really?"

"No."

"What does the word 'Jew' mean, then, in your efficient lexicon? It appears after the phrase 'not admitted' in your pamphlet."

Dewey stammered meaninglessly as he tried to recover his equilibrium, but Dr. Michelson waved him off. "Tonight's events were entertaining, and perhaps even temporarily useful in terms of stopping the antics of some of this state's criminalized politicians, but in the long term, I suspect that, even with the help of your carnival worker here, this evening will have been a waste of everyone's time."

Dr. Michelson turned on his heel and walked outside to the guest parking lot.

With him walked away Dewey's opportunity to woo Governor Roosevelt toward the metric system via Dr. Michelson. Dewey had made a mistake from the beginning. He, unlike Miss Shaw, knew that personal charm was key to any kind of conversion. Unfortunately, Dr. Michelson had little susceptibility to charm to begin with, making him a hard case for a man like Dewey. An arrest with the promise of

Miss Shaw doing a cooch show (that had been what Dewey had promised, she had guessed, to these eminent men) was not conducive to creating goodwill with the light specialist. As often happened, Dewey's penchant for multitasking had backfired.

Dewey stared unhappily at Dr. Michelson's departing bulk, but eventually he recovered himself and addressed Miss Shaw. "As usual, I want to know how you did it."

"In the coatroom, I found in Mr. Avenmore's pocket a key-ring with a horseshoe bauble and a ticket from a church raffle in support of an orphanage well-provisioned by other Tammany Hall politicians. The key-ring was made of gold, and the wallet of kid leather. He loved the finer things, yet he could not shake off his perceived duty to his religion, which, despite his surname's Anglo-Saxon flavour, is obviously papist. The horseshoe was not made of gold. It was of cheap metal. It was worn down with much rubbing, which means that despite his religiosity he did not forgo a belief in lucky charms. Our Regent has had many occasions to rub his horseshoe while invoking a higher power (Christian or not). Someone implicated with graft, blackmail and conspiracy, and yet in conflict with himself over it, might often seek supernatural solace."

Dewey shook his head. "Admirable."

"The rest was just research. Once I saw the contents of his pocket I knew he would be an easy mark."

"Yes, it went fairly well." He managed an unconvincing grin.

Untrue: it had gone well in some ways and not in others. Neither of them had to say this out loud, however. They knew each other too well.

"I must go home," Dewey said. "My wife will wonder about my whereabouts."

That was code for Mrs. Dewey's suspicions that he fornicated with other women. Never had that other woman been Miss Shaw.

Very deeply, Dewey bowed to Miss Shaw. "Until next time."

She waited until she saw his dark figure round another building and disappear in the direction of his private residence. She left the building too, then, oblivious to the few hangers-on who watched and wondered. Around her lay the residue of the evening's events, people in groups of two or three or four, loitering outside their cabins and gawking at the final departing police wagon fading down the road in the dark twinkling of early night. The night's entertainment was finished.

She recalled Dewey's parting words. If there was a next time. Dewey's eccentricity and egocentricity had forced him to flee Columbia University before it could toss him out. How long before he received the same treatment in Albany?

Now she would have to make her own way home. Dewey wouldn't let her stay at Lake Placid Club. She was part gypsy and part Jewish, after all. In any event, her presence here might alert people to her centrality in Dewey's life-plans, and she needed to remain on the sidelines. Within decent walking distance on the other side of Mirror Lake lived a Romany family she knew who would help her return to Albany.

Dewey used her. She understood that. She used him

too. No matter how many libraries he organized, decimal systems he implemented or spellings he reformed, he was like a carnie. As did most carnies, she and he would both land on their feet.

She composed herself and began her walk toward the moon.

I Will Not Let You Fall

by Linda Webber

After the short story 'I Will Not Let You Fall', creating this bio has been the greatest challenge to Linda's creative writing skills. This is her first publication, even though she has written a great deal of fiction (five short stories). Although one story did receive praise from her writing group (not 'I Will Not Let You Fall'), another story did not receive as much. Linda's writing career spans nine months; therefore, she is hoping to publish something else any day now.

I peer over the computer to look at Isabelle without her noticing me. Her adorable face convinces me nothing is wrong.

Isabelle is looking at picture books with the other kids. She's the one wearing the Pepto-Bismol pink shirt and pants, and shiny pink shoes. Isabelle is trying to decipher what must, to her, be meaningless squiggles. Her sandy blond pigtails bob up and down as she pretends to read. When she discovers the next page, Isabelle's azure blue eyes widen and her chubby cheeks become a deeper shade of red. Her amazement is only momentary, and the sparkly buttons on her sweater become more fascinating than the book. She sees me. I duck behind the computer, too late.

"Ma!" Isabelle screams. Her short, pudgy legs pound across the floor. She resembles a giant wad of bubble gum racing towards me.

"Use your inside voice," I whisper.

"Ma look, I can read," she yells at the book and everyone in the library. "Hat in a cat." Her stubby fingers crush the pages.

"Shhh, it says 'Cat in the Hat'." I point to each word as I read slowly.

Her lower lip protrudes and she meanders back to her little chair with her head down. In grade three, she still can't even read the title. I hide behind the computer to stop the people who are staring.

3.1 per 100 births, the article says. *It is the leading cause of birth defects and mental deficiency.*

I glance at Isabelle's eager and faultless face. Things I forgot existed excite her: broccoli trees, "curly" whirlwinds of dust, and "sparkly" rain. Between soul-mutilating bills and loads of laundry, she reminds me that I am alive.

Maybe they're wrong. The psychologist said she has an average IQ. It's only sometimes that she does stupid things. She was so proud of her Santa panties, she lifted her dress to show the audience of two hundred at this year's Christmas concert. She's just impulsive.

None of the adults were able to live independently or to maintain employment.

The doctor must be wrong. She has to be wrong. There is a tremendous crash. Isabelle wails. Pink arms and legs flail under a toppled display. I race to her. A man is helping her up. I hold Isabelle, rock her, and stroke her head. Her plump little arms cling to me, trembling. Her tears soak my chest.

"Are you okay? What happened Isabelle?"

"She tried to climb the display," the man says.

"I wanted a high-up book." Isabelle scrunches her nose and glares at the overturned display that attacked her.

I love her and I want to strangle her. She is eight years old and she terrifies me. I swallow.

"Let's help pick up the books and then you can go to the craft group."

Isabelle flings books onto the display rack.

"Careful," I say as Isabelle sprints to the craft room.

Now maybe I can get ten undisturbed minutes to read before we go to the bank, the laundromat, and the grocery store.

Many children forgot how to perform basic tasks, only to remember and then forget again, a few moments later, an article reports.

A familiar sobbing approaches.

"They kicked me out," howls Isabelle with outstretched arms.

I embrace her. Her desperate heart pounds against my breast. When I kiss her sweaty hysterical head, she smells of crayons, clay, and snot.

"What's in your ears?" I ask.

"Earrings. We made clay stuff."

"You shoved clay in your ears?"

"Yeah," Isabelle says. "And I made nose rings."

She grins and tips her head back to show me her clay-packed nostrils. I feel my stomach contract. I cannot speak. I want to shake her and scream, but she beams, oblivious.

After visiting the bathroom and cleaning out the clay, I put Isabelle in the little chair beside me with her book. Isabelle imagines she is reading 'Hat in a Cat'. I must watch her. When she was born, I put bows in her curls and everyone admired her. My co-workers gave me their second-hand stuff.

I need to stop reminiscing and focus on these articles. *Early signs include learning and behaviour issues, inattention, distractibility, and impulsivity.*

When I look up the chair is empty. I scan the library. I cannot see her. I search the bathroom, the craft room, and the study carrels. She is nowhere. Gone. Isabelle is gone.

I rush to the information desk. My hands and legs are trembling. Blood has drained from my body. I see a stack of encyclopedias under a table. A wee pink shoe peeks out, then two pigtails.

"Ma, I made a fort!" yells Isabelle.

I want to disown her. I want to run. Tears run streaming running down my face.

"Ma, what's wrong? Do you gots a owie?" Isabelle says. She rushes to comfort me, hugging my waist and patting my butt.

"I love you," she says.

I am laughing and crying at the same time. I gulp down my sobs and pick up my precious treasure. Her delicate breath tickles my face. Her warm stickiness melds into me the way it does when she crawls into my bed early in the morning smelling of Halloween candy and play-doh. We rock together in time with the ABC song Isabelle hums, until I become aware of the time.

"Let's put the books back. We only have a few more minutes. And, this time, stay here," I say, pointing to the small chair. "Don't move."

The pattern of alcohol consumption most likely to result in Fetal Alcohol Spectrum Disorder is binge drinking in the first trimester.

My heart pounds and races as if it's trying to escape. My breathing stops, and my body is a numb shell I no longer inhabit. The library becomes a distant, quiet fuzz, as if I am alone, weightless, suspended without anchor in time and place. The keyboard under my fingertips and the chair I sit on disappear.

There is a tugging sensation on my arm. "…this say?"

"What?"

"What does this say, Ma?"

"Don't bother me."

Isabelle's head drops. She hides behind her book.

A woman sitting at the computer across the table jerks her head up to look at me.

"You wanna read to her?" I ask the woman whose head jerks back to her computer.

Goddamn people who judge. I know they're all judging. Goddamn people. Goddamn library. Screw all of you. And screw that goddamn son-of-a-bitch Derrick. I was almost glad when that jerk left me alone, broke, 6,000 miles from home, and three months pregnant. They can all go to hell.

A melodic cadence pulls me back to the present.

"Cat in the Hat," Isabelle says, following the words with her stubby finger.

" *'Have no fear!' said the cat.*
'I will not let you fall.
I will hold you up high

As I stand on a ball.'" [1]

Isabelle looks up at me, the gap between her two front teeth exposed, traces of a jelly sandwich under her chin. My heart explodes. I clutch Isabelle to me and stroke her small head. My angel finally read the little words. Maybe if we try hard enough, maybe I can teach her, maybe she can learn how to wash her face, how to cross streets, and how to make sandwiches. She might get it.

She snuggles into my lap, resting her body against mine. "Read, Mommy."

I struggle to control my faltering voice as I read,

" *'With a book on one hand!*
And a cup on my hat!
But that is not All I can do!'
Said the cat …'" [1]

"Yeah! We can read. Let's get ice cream," Isabelle says, standing on her chair and shrieking to the shoppers in the mall past the library doors.

Isabelle lunges from her chair as though someone has fired a starting gun for an obstacle course through the library. She topples children who block her shortest route, rams a cart into a display creating an explosion of CD cases, vaults over a computer desk, and smashes into the glass wall beside the exit. The wailing, once again, commences. I grab our bags and race after her.

1. The Cat in the Hat, Dr. Seuss, Random House, New York, 1975.

Library Lost

by M. L. Kulmatycki

M. Lea Kulmatycki is a teacher and writer. Her work spans academic writing to a senior's advice column in a local newspaper. She has even written poetry for some charitable events. After many years of writing and publishing teaching materials, she decided to focus on her first love, fiction. She is also on the board of directors of the Young Alberta Book Society.

———————————

I wasn't being brave. Just curious. Or maybe fed up with the old man's stories. Whether it was an effort to prove him wrong so he'd shut up or the hope that he was right was anyone's guess.

I'd been careful. But the soft click followed by the barely audible hum said otherwise. I leaned against the cold remnants of what had once been an intricately carved stone-wall surrounding an inner courtyard. I hugged my knees tight, wishing I could disappear. The sentry had started his rounds earlier than usual. I could hear his footsteps in the distance heading my way. I slowed my breathing to minimize the faint mist produced with each exhalation as it combined with the night air.

Of more concern was the smell of sweat that clung to my t-shirt under the greatcoat. Crawling across broken rooftops and scrabbling through streets from one discarded piece of building to another in the inner city core was more taxing than I had anticipated. I should have wrapped the greatcoat around my waist, but it would have been too bulky. The owner I'd scavenged it from definitely wasn't a teenage girl. I couldn't save him, but I still felt guilty that I took the coat.

They called themselves the Pleth. Their physiology was so close to human, the differences went unnoticed for a long time. It had been simpler to believe humankind was somehow related to this race from the stars than question their true origins. Questions about their home planet or history were met with vague answers, anyhow. Only a handful of reporters had noted the absence of females among the Pleth ambassadors. Having little knowledge of Pleth culture, their comments were ignored by the human representatives for fear of offending the Pleth.

When the Pleth arrived, they'd offered peace and technology not seen since before the Descent. The seduction of regaining the knowledge lost during the Anti-tech Crusades had been too alluring. Earth's planetary government had welcomed the Pleth as long lost brothers. The war had been close to lost when the people who were supposed to know everything realized they knew nothing.

The Pleth weren't human. And they hadn't come in peace. It wasn't until the war that autopsies of their fallen soldiers revealed three lungs and a double heart. They had been careful to conceal the thin ear slits in front of their ears with a helmet or hair. But it was their extraordinary sense of smell which had been humanity's fall. It would be the end of my existence if the sentry picked up my scent.

The footsteps stopped on the other side of the wall.

The Pleth were no longer as careful as they'd been in the beginning, because it was no longer necessary. I imagined the Pleth a few meters away on the other side of the wall, inhaling deeply and testing the air for the rancid stench of human. I held my breath.

A soft click followed by the fading hum of the Pleth's weapon signaled safety. I breathed a soft sigh of relief. The Pleth hadn't smelt my sweat, but instead the plants and waste I'd rubbed all over my greatcoat. I had spent hours hidden on the rooftop across from the building the old man called The Library. I had successfully identified many of the plants and the waste within its crumbling courtyard. I had been able to locate those same plants and waste in safer areas of the city to use for the concoction smeared on the greatcoat.

I stared at the broken building at the other end of the courtyard. Crumpled and long dead, savagely battered in comparison to the surrounding derelict buildings, it fit with the old man's stories. It hadn't been a victim of the Pleth bombings. The Library had died long ago in the Anti-tech Crusades.

The jagged bits of building poking up at the night sky seemed the best point of entry. There was no guarantee they were anything more than parts of a wall or perhaps a column. But I had a feeling, and that was better than nothing. If I was wrong, I figured there was enough room under the fallen stone to hide during the day, and I could retrace my steps back to the tunnels the following evening. I didn't need much room.

I'm thin, skin and bones thin. The above-grounders and Pleth call us tunnel rats for good reason. Nothing grows in the abandoned subway tunnels we call home and we scavenge for every morsel of food. But it's a better fate than most.

If there wasn't an opening under the pile of debris or enough room to conceal me for the day, I wouldn't be the only one to die. The Pleth would purge the tunnels in the district, killing everyone they could find. They would call it a lesson. The above-grounders wouldn't care. After all, us tunnel rats are just vermin. Not wealthy enough, not smart enough, and not connected enough. I sometimes wondered if the above-grounders recognized the prison they had created for themselves living under Pleth rule.

The moon, a mere sliver of light, was in my favor. My time in the tunnels had improved my night vision. Besides, a palm light attracted trouble and was a luxury not to be wasted. The technology and knowledge to repair them was lost long ago.

It took most of the evening to work my way across the courtyard, slipping from the shadows of one pile of rubble to another. I slid feet first into the small gap in the side of the pile of rubble I figured hid the entrance to The Library, the building now just a mound of debris surrounded by a collapsing stone wall.

I was right. Overlapping, cracked concrete slabs formed a small dome and the ghostly light shining through holes here and there revealed an opening at the end opposite me.

I scrambled closer to the dark pit. As wide as two grown men, it could have been five meters deep or fifty-five. The darkness was like black water in a well. I couldn't see that changing in daylight and I couldn't risk a palm light. The same slits that lit the small space surrounding the hole would betray my presence.

In one of the pockets in my greatcoat I had carefully coiled a dirth rope. Its thinness disguised its strength. The fine hook at the end of the coil could catch onto substances that seemed as smooth as glass. It was Pleth. I had come by it the same way I had my greatcoat and many other possessions. Survival had taught me not to be squeamish.

I placed the hook at the edge of the hole and tugged to reassure myself it would hold. I slid onto my stomach, grabbed the rope, and lowered myself feet first down into the black pit.

The jagged rock wall made for easy footholds. The dim circle of light at the top of the pit was still clearly visible as I worked my way down. I relaxed and fell into the rhythm of searching out one foothold, then another. I figured I would get to the bottom in no time.

A loud crack startled me. Small bits of stone sprinkled down from the top of the pit. Within moments, a hailstorm of debris rained down on me. I raised one hand to shield my head and clung to the rope as I was buffeted against the sides of the pit. Little good it did me as pieces of rubble struck my head and scratched my face. A trickle of warmth worked its way down my cheek. Each side of my body was smashed successively against the wall, like a twig tossed in the wind. Then the hook on the dirth rope did the impossible. It slid off the lip of the hole with a hideous scraping sound.

I awoke in a sprawl on my back with my forehead throbbing. I couldn't remember hitting the ground and had no idea how far I had fallen. There was no way of telling how long I had lain unconscious in the inky nothingness. My hunger wasn't an adequate measure. I was always hungry. The dirth rope lay on top of me. I gingerly tested my limbs, checking for injuries. My body ached all over and I felt a lump near my temple. The small gash below was crusted over with blood. Thankfully I was still able to move.

I winced as I re-coiled the dirth rope. I stuck it in a pocket in my greatcoat, then dug a palm light out of another pocket. Focusing my thoughts on the palm light, I watched as it slowly floated upwards. A soft glow surrounded me. I had room to stand up.

The pit had caved in, blocking out any remnants of light from the outside world. Judging by the pieces of concrete sticking up at odd angles, the pit had, at one time, been a stairwell. Surrounded by debris on three sides, there was only one direction to go. Palm light floating beside my shoulder, I picked my way into the darkness.

Broken slabs of stone gradually gave way to smooth walls covered in grime. Cautious, I wanted to leave as little trace of my presence as possible, so avoided touching the walls. The downward pull on my legs meant the passageway was gradually taking me further underground. Not much later, the walls on either side of me dissolved into darkness.

An eerie glow began to diffuse the black around me as I walked on with wobbly feet. I turned off my palm light and let my eyes adjust so that I could spy the other source of light.

Above and in front of me were glow globes embedded in metal poles. Pieces of fallen ceiling had bent many of the poles into macabre shapes. Decades later, the glow globes on some of them still functioned, casting light along the floor where they lay. I kept moving toward them and saw more glow globes embedded in the broken, high ceiling. Less than half worked. My field of vision grew with the light and I saw rows upon rows of narrow metal shelves that stood like soldiers. Some had tipped over, falling on adjacent ones and causing a chain reaction of tipped shelves. Interspersed beside the shelves in small groups were tables of all sizes. Chairs were scattered here and there, but a few remained nestled under the tables as if time had stood still.

I walked toward the row of shelves closest to me, startled by the crunch of my boots. I bent down. Shards of glass, dust and grit covered the floor like a carpet. Dark boxes, split open or mangled as the shelves had fallen, lay among the mess. In many of the untouched shelves rows of the dark boxes were arranged side by side.

I picked up the nearest box and lifted the lid. Inside, four rows of thin glass slides remained intact. Info-slides. I smiled and shook my head. It didn't make sense. According to the old man, all The Libraries were destroyed by the Anti-techs during the Crusades before the Descent. It wasn't until the Post-Descent era that mankind had understood the loss of the knowledge that could have rebuilt the destroyed technology and avoided civilization's plunge into anarchy.

Decades of darkness were followed by the rise of the rich. Their bits and pieces of technology that still functioned had been salvaged. It didn't take them long to rebuild their elegant structures that rose into the air, leaving the rest of humanity to scrape out a meager existence in the slums built out of the remains of decaying buildings destroyed by the Crusades and riots. While the earth's population had diminished, the needs of the wealthy and privileged had not. It surprised me that someone had not investigated the ruin near the middle of what had once been a major center, but maybe it had been overlooked during a brief period where the rich appetite was sated.

The info-slides would be worthless without functioning readers. I crouched and hurried under the shelves and down the long aisles, afraid the glow globes would suddenly go out. The metal shelves loomed over me as if watching and waiting.

Nothing. Not one reader. If the room had been purged by the anti-techs, then I should have found destroyed readers scattered throughout. Unless I wasn't looking in the right place.

What had I missed? I stood on one of the big tables in front of the rows of shelves and carefully scrutinized everything I could see. I hopped from table to table, repeating my scan until I reached the end of the room. Tall thin cupboards jutted out of the walls in regular intervals.

I ran to the closest cupboard and opened the doors. A tangle of broken readers slid out onto my boots. Whether it was the vibrations from the bombings of the Crusades, the Pleth war, or both, the readers had not survived. I left the mess and ran to the next cupboard. A second avalanche of broken readers.

Cupboard after cupboard of mangled readers slid onto the floor. It didn't stop until I reached the seventh cupboard and was greeted by six rows of slim metal rectangles snuggled into slots that ran the length of each shelf. Thirty-six readers. I continued cupboard to cupboard. Four cupboards untouched. One hundred forty-four readers intact. But did they function? Almost one hundred years had passed since anyone might have been in this place.

Armed with a handful of readers and a box of info-slides, I set to work. Wiping off a space on one of the long tables, I placed four of the readers and four info-slides in front of me. I was convinced I could figure out how they worked. The unit automatically turned on when an info-slide was inserted into the slit at the top. It took a while to realize there was a distinctive click when the info-slide was correctly in place. The info-slide projected a holographic image of one written page. I had just about given up trying to figure out how to turn the page when my hand brushed the corner of the projected page and the next page appeared. I wasn't sure if the tears I wept were from joy or fatigue. I lost track of time as I discovered how to navigate my way through the info-slide by tapping and dragging my finger along various parts of the holographic page. It was even possible to tap on an image and a three-dimensional colored image was projected above the page. It was a simple, but impressive piece of technology. I tested each reader, stacking the ones that worked at one end of the table, returning those that didn't to the cupboards.

My stomach rumbled after I had gone through the stacks of readers. I dug into a pocket of my greatcoat and pulled out a stale military food bar and water tube. I stared at the one hundred and three fully functioning readers. The next step would be to figure out the contents of the unbroken info-slides. The old man had talked about stories, factual information, as well as info-slides that chronicled the history of the human race. More importantly, he said there had been info-slides explaining the lost tech-knowledge. He said the ancient knowledge could defeat the Pleth.

I carried the first intact box of info-slides to the table and took a deep breath. Yes, I could read. In more than one language, the two main languages used for global communication, Pleth and English, a few less common languages as well as a couple that died with their race. My mother had been insistent on it. Said it would be the difference between life and death. She had been right. I whispered a thank you to her.

It was not long before I realized the magnitude of my find. These weren't stories to entertain. Page after page of schematics projected in front of me. I tapped on the images and they were replaced by tiny holographic replicas of machines I had never seen before. This was tech-knowledge. Detailed tech-knowledge. It mattered little if the information built something great or something small. Someone would know what to do with it. Was it possible that all the information in The Library was tech-knowledge? It would take weeks to look at each info-slide to find out.

The writing on any of The Library's signs that may have given me clues had long ago faded away. However, I noticed that the shelves were arranged in groups. I decided to select a few info-slides from each shelf within each group with the hope they contained similar information.

At the end of what I estimated to be a couple of days, I knew I had a big problem. Ninety percent of the slides were intact and they all contained information that would change the world. Tech-knowledge. And I didn't think I was the only one who knew this. Someone had deliberately brought the info- slides into this part of The Library in an effort to hide them.

I hadn't slept much while I worked, worried that the power to the glow globes would shut down before I finished my task. Instead, I took breaks to keep myself focused and I explored the destruction beyond the room. I wanted to see if I could find a way out. One of the outer rooms was filled with less debris than the others and I was convinced the room marked the way out. It took quite a bit of time to discover the hole in the wall that had been cleverly hidden by a pile of furniture. I was certain I had a way out. That seemed insignificant compared to the information I pieced together.

The room full of shelves was the central hub, with other rooms branching off. The occasional undamaged info- slide I found in the other rooms told a story of a group of people moving all the tech info into the one room, a last minute decision done with haste. The outer ring of rooms had been bombed from within, sealing off the central room. This hidden sanctuary was someone's desperate gamble to save the human race. I knew they'd wanted the information hidden with the hope that sometime in the future, the room would be found and its value understood.

I had discovered all The Library had to offer. I slipped twelve info-slides carefully wrapped in my spare T-shirt, along with three readers, into my greatcoat. I left the room knowing I would be back.

The journey out wasn't as treacherous as the journey down. The building had shifted several times over the years, which made parts of the passageway I followed difficult. Had I been a grown man, I might not have been able to wriggle through some of the gaps in the walls. I could feel the encouragement of a steady incline, and that kept me going through the hunger and exhaustion.

The tunnel gradually widened and then stopped abruptly, blocked by a pile of rocks. In front of me the walls had collapsed. Light poked through here and there between the stones barricading my way, taunting me. I scrambled upward, squatted at the top of the heap, and scrutinized the individual rocks as if they were pieces of a puzzle. If I removed the wrong ones, ceiling and walls could start to shift and crumble.

Gradually, a sound beyond the rocks interrupted my thoughts. Faint, but distinct. Snakes. A lot of snakes. There must have been a nest on the other side of the cave-in. I had seen snakes leaving their homes in the ruins in the city at the end of the cold season. Hundreds of them had spilt into the deserted streets in search of food and warmth. I knew it wasn't uncommon for snakes to make their nests in openings on the side of a hill. There was no way I could get through safely.

I thought about going back, then remembered that I would be stuck at the caved-in pit that had led me here in the first place.

Cursing, I stood in the middle of the tunnel, palm light illuminating my only escape route. Staring at the blocked passage, my breath caught. Was I seeing things? The rocks seemed to make a regular pattern. Was this a deliberate attempt to hide the exit? Or was it an attempt to seal an unwanted entrance? I began to doubt that the snakes were a simple coincidence. A deterrent perhaps? There had to be an entrance known to the people behind this deception, maybe only used when they deemed the time right. Unfortunately, I was certain this was not the time.

I sat down, back against the cool, rough stone, and sighed heavily. Deliberate or not, it made no difference. I would die here if I could not find an exit. I had told no one of my plan to enter The Library. All of my sisters were elsewhere, preoccupied with Resistance efforts in the cities further south. I was still too young to help with the dangerous sabotage missions.

Taynea lived with me in the tunnels, but she had left a few days ago and had been vague about when she would return. I had not pressed the issue. My sisters were adept at deflecting my questions so they always went unanswered. At times, I wondered why the Sisterhood had chosen to join the Resistance, an organization led by men. Surely, there were other means of achieving the Sisterhood's goals than to tie ourselves to men once again.

Then I thought about the old man. It hadn't been simple pride that had kept me from telling him, my desire to prove him wrong. I didn't trust him. I had seen too many strangers coming and going from his room. But that was no cause for mistrust.

I felt guilty admitting my feelings because there was no reason for me not to trust the kindly old man. Everyone in the tunnels called him "Grandfather." Long before I had made the tunnels my home, the old man had accepted the leadership of the ragtag family that lived there.

Taynea had been living in the tunnels for several months before I joined her. Repected and admired by everyone she met, she was everything I aspired to be. Strong and fearless, but kind. I was certain it was because of her that Grandfather had treated me well and accepted me without question into his flock of children.

There was no way forward, so my only option was to try and find another way. I stood up and retraced my steps, looking carefully for any stone, crack, or shadow that might indicate a hidden exit. I was halfway back to the hidden room when I spotted a pinprick of light at the bottom of a wall. Moving my palm light closer, I saw that the grime of a century had effectively camouflaged a faint rectangular indent much wider and slightly taller than myself.

I felt along the outline. No hinges, no handles. I placed my hands in the middle and pushed. Nothing. Then the top and bottom. Same result. I was positive there was a mechanism controlling the door. I continued pushing at the door in various places. Finally, there was a grinding sound and the block of stone slid quietly back, leaving enough space to squeeze through the opening.

The light burned my eyes. I dropped to my knees. The contrast to the darkness underground was almost unbearable. It was a while before my head stopped aching and I could see clearly. I was in an alcove on the exterior of a fallen building. The debris covering the opening concealed it, and me, from prying eyes. I doubted this was a coincidence.

While I couldn't be seen, it was impossible for me to see anything other than the blank wall of another building. There were no clues to indicate the location of the tunnel's exit. I was forced to patiently wait for dusk to minimize the risk of being seen as I left the alcove.

As darkness fell, I crept around the building and climbed onto the roof. I needed to make sure nothing had changed and that my usual routes would take me safely out of the inner city core. Across the street was The Library. The tunnel that led me here had more than likely been a part of the subway system.

The moon shone in the night sky and lit up The Library. My problem was much bigger than getting back to my home in the tunnels unseen. Believing anything that remained of the The Library was inaccessible, the bombed carcass from the Anti-Tech Crusades had been left untouched during the Pleth raids. What had changed their minds? I hadn't been trapped by a cave-in. The Pleth had bombed the ruins of The Library.

I don't believe in coincidence. The dirth rope hadn't slipped and the bombing of the ruins was deliberate. The Pleth knew I had entered The Library. I was in possession of a commodity someone had carefully hidden. Something the Pleth didn't want found. I prayed the Pleth didn't know I had been successful.

Who had told them? Life in the tunnels was nothing more than day-to-day survival. I had left many times to explore. At times, I had been gone for three or four days. No one had noticed or cared.

Except one person: the old man. Could he have told me the stories knowing my curiosity would send me in search of the info-slides? Tech-knowledge could help the Resistance in the fight against the Pleth. Who better for the job than an expendable teenage girl? But how did the Pleth find out what I was attempting to do?

I included a detour as I slipped from one shadow to another, heading back to my home in the tunnels. I had a hiding place in the wild area, the edge of the city, in a ruin that had been long forgotten.

Few wandered beyond the core of the city. It was dangerous. Occasionally, Pleth scouts checked the area for the Resistance and packs of feral animals scavenged for food, the land beyond a toxic wasteland created during the Pleth war. Despite the strict rules the old man had in place, I left nothing of worth in my room in the tunnels. I placed all but one reader and an info-slide in my hiding place. I needed to find out who wanted me dead.

I headed to the tunnels. It was past midnight when I walked casually up to the entrance as if returning from one of my exploring expeditions.

"Oriole!" A shadow came running out of the tunnel to greet me. The light revealed eight-year-old Ben's dirt-covered, worried face. "Where have you been?"

"Exploring," I replied, surprised anyone had noticed my absence.

"Where?" Ben asked, grabbing my hand and tugging me into the entry of the tunnel.

"Shouldn't you be in bed?" I asked, hoping to divert the boy's attention.

"Mom thinks I am," he said, "but I knew you were just exploring."

"Ben." I stopped, ignoring the tugs on my hand. "What's going on? I've left the tunnels before."

He looked at me far too seriously for a child his age. "Don't you know?"

"Know what?"

"The Pleth, Oriole," Ben replied. "There were bombs. In the center of the city. After, the Pleth raided the tunnels. They killed Solange and her dad. No one could find you. Grandfather said the Pleth must have got you too. But I told him he was wrong. I told him he forgot, but he said he didn't know what I was talking about. I don't lie, Oriole. I knew what I was talking about. I saw you."

The words tumbled out of Ben so fast it was hard to put the pieces together. A Pleth raid? Nothing of significance had occurred in the tunnels to warrant a Pleth raid. The bombing would keep the tech-knowledge hidden. Why would the Pleth raid the tunnels? There was much more going on.

"Of course you don't lie, Ben," I said. "Why would Grandfather think you were lying?"

Ben just shrugged his shoulders. "Don't know. I followed you just like he said."

"When did Grandfather ask you to follow me?" I asked.

"When you started going into the core. You know, Oriole. When you were staying on the roofs of those buildings, spying on someone."

I didn't know if I was more disturbed that the old man had me followed or that I hadn't noticed Ben. But then I reminded myself that tunnel rats learned early in life how to survive. "Why did Grandfather ask you to follow me?"

"Dunno," replied Ben. "Just did. That's why I knew you weren't in the tunnels. You were out spying again."

"No, Ben." I laughed, trying to pretend the whole thing was amusing. "I wasn't spying. I was just curious and figuring something out."

"What?" Ben asked.

I paused for a moment. It was obvious the old man knew what I had been doing. I needed a simple explanation if I was going to carry through my plan. An explanation I could share openly so it would appear to be the truth.

"Grandfather keeps telling stories about The Library," I began. Ben nodded in agreement. "I wanted to find out if any of them were true."

Ben nodded again, pursing his lips and trying to look older and wiser. "So did you find anything?"

"I couldn't even get near the place." I sighed, trying to sound disappointed. "The Pleth were everywhere. I was on one of the rooftops the night they bombed the place. I was worried they were watching. I didn't want to lead them back here. So, I spent some time in the wild area. I figured the Pleth wouldn't bother following me in there."

"You could have got hurt, Oriole," Ben said, and hugged me.

"But I wasn't," I whispered, hoping my story would satisfy Ben and any others he would tell.

"Are you gonna tell Grandfather?" Ben asked, pulling away to look me in the eyes. "He'll be disappointed."

"Ya," I replied. "But at least he'll know I tried to find proof that his stories are true. I'm going to see if he's still up."

"Can I come, Oriole?" Ben asked.

"Sorry, Ben," I said, shaking my head. "Past your bedtime. Now scoot back to bed before your mom notices you're missing. I'll tell you everything later."

"Promise?"

"Promise," I replied. "Go on now. I'll see you in the morning."

"I missed you, Oriole." Ben grabbed me and gave me another hug, then abruptly ran away down the tunnel.

"Ben," I shouted after him, "is Taynea back?"

"Nope," he yelled.

I wished that Taynea had returned. She would know what to do. I knew the Sisterhood had spies everywhere. They would know who was behind the bombing of The Library and how to retrieve the rest of the info-slides and readers. I strode down the tunnel to the old man's room.

Amare and Daquon, part of the old man's entourage, were smoking a cylinder of rog outside his door. The drug was common in the tunnels. It gave the illusion of meaning to the day-to-day existence.

I had never given it much thought, but there were always a couple of men outside the old man's door. Guess he felt he needed protection. Today, for some reason, the guards stuck out, probably because I knew they'd give me trouble. Or maybe because I was nervous.

"Oriole," Amare said as I approached, "everyone thought the Pleth gotcha. Suppose you were out doing your exploring." He laughed, his speech slightly slurred, and moved to block the entrance. Most of the people living in our tunnel thought my exploring was foolish. But most of them had stopped living a long time ago. "What d'ya want?"

"Need to see the old man," I replied.

"I suppose you found something important on your

exploring," he said again.

"It's late, Oriole," Daquon said, joining Amare in front of the door. "Go home and come back in the morning. He's old. He needs sleep."

"You're right, Amare. I have something for him," I said.

"Show us and we'll decide if we need to wake him up," Amare said, as if he was daring me to prove my exploring was useful, not an excuse to hide from the realities of the tunnel.

"It's not for you, Amare," I said, knowing the two men had shared more than one cylinder and could be trouble. "It's for the old man. He told me to bring it to him. If you don't let me pass, you know what he'll do."

The old man had always appeared kind and gentle, but if my gut feeling was right, this was simply a mask for those not involved in his affairs. It was a gamble, but I needed to get past the old man's bodyguards. I knew I had been right when neither one wanted to make that decision.

The door burst open and the decision was taken from them. The old man appeared in the doorway. The commotion had awoken him. Dressed in thin pants, a ragged t-shirt, and bare feet, he looked worn and tired. His long greying hair, usually worn loose and flowing, was tied back at the nape of his neck.

"Oriole!" the old man shouted as he grabbed and hugged me. He held on to my arm and ushered me into his room. He pointed to a threadbare armchair in his living area and sat down on the matching sofa across from me. A beaded curtain separated his sleeping area from the living area and office. The placement of furniture marked the boundaries between his personal space and office space. "Everyone thought you were dead."

"So I've heard," I replied, trying to ignore the relief I heard in his voice for fear I would stop the charade I had planned.

"Where were you?" he asked.

"The Library," I replied. "I decided to try and find some of those readers and info-slides you keep telling us about in your stories."

"The risk, Oriole, the risk," the old man said in a pained voice. "Why would you put yourself at such risk?"

"I thought you would be pleased," I replied, feigning confusion. The old man appeared to be truly upset.

"Pleased that you put your life in jeopardy?" he said tersely. "Oriole, the Pleth bombed The Library days ago. You could have been hurt or killed!"

"But I wasn't," I said, pretending to be ignorant of the dangers of my journey and excited about what I brought back. "Look, the slides don't work. But your stories—your stories are true. Look."

I stood up and walked over to the sofa. I sat down beside him and handed him the broken reader and pieces of info-slide that I had put in a pocket of my greatcoat. I hoped I hadn't destroyed them for nothing.

He stared at them for a moment. "Proof was not worth risking your life."

A small piece of the info-slide slipped off his hand and tinkled as it hit the floor, shattering.

"So fragile," he said as he bent down to pick up the broken fragments.

"They were all broken. Your beautiful stories were all broken." I sighed and bent down to help.

As I handed the old man two fragments of the info slide, I looked up at him, hoping I looked innocent and mournful. I wanted to be sure.

Carelessness is a death wish, and the old man had been careless. He had pulled his hair into the tail at the nape of his neck before going to sleep thinking no one would notice the faint scar in front of each ear.

For a moment, all I could focus on were the two thin lines. I recognized them for what they were. Ear slit scars. Pleth military surgery for undercover work. My guilt for thinking I had misjudged him was swallowed by the icy rage of survival.

He looked at me, the façade of the kindly, old man melting away as he realized his mistake. He stood up and looked down at me, his cold, hard eyes betraying himself. In their depths I saw that he knew me for what I was. The corner of his mouth turned up in a sneer, daring me to deny the truth. Before he could offer any explanations, any more lies, I slipped the fine steel skewer hidden inside my boot and punctured the old man's right heart and then his left. He sagged to the floor like a wilted flower. I knelt beside him, feeling used and betrayed.

"I'm not the one to fear," he said. Then he died.

As I wiped off the blade on a piece of the old man's clothing and slipped it back into my boot, there was a commotion at the door. I heard raised voices before the door flung open.

"Oriole," Taynea exclaimed as she closed the door and

crossed the room. The laughter in her eyes turned to anger when she saw the blood on the old man's chest. Her smile quickly faded and her lips pressed together.

"I'm so glad you're back." I threw myself at her, relief flooding my body, knowing she would understand.

Taynea pushed me aside as she walked over to the old man crumpled on the floor. Her voice stern and accusing, she asked, "What have you done?"

"He's Pleth, Taynea," I said.

"I know," she replied, her face cold and emotionless, as if his death was just an inconvenience. "The other members of the Resistance know. We found him more useful alive than dead. It's a pity you killed him."

"I didn't know. You weren't here," I stammered. I didn't want her to be angry with me.

Taynea turned to me, the dead body on the floor forgotten for the moment. "I just arrived and spoke to Ben on my way here. How did you get out of The Library?"

Grandfather had been right. He was not the one to fear. It was one of my sisters. The person I loved, admired, respected. She had been willing to let me die. Taynea had used me and thought nothing of it. She had betrayed me and the Sisterhood. She was a spy, a Pletha prolonging the tyranny of our Pleth oppressors, hiding the knowledge that would raise us from the ashes.

I looked at Taynea, tears sliding down my face. Before she could offer a lie to explain how she knew I had been trapped in The Library, I drew the metal skewer from my boot and punctured Taynea's right heart, then her left. I placed the skewer in her hand.

97

"Amare! Daquon!" I shouted. By now the cylinders should have dulled their thinking enough for me to easily manipulate their account of what happened. The old man had tried to kill Taynea and she had managed to kill him before she died. I would make sure everyone was aware of the important role Amare and Daquon played in the two deaths. Tomorrow, they would gladly accept the accolades rather than admitting they could recall little. The evening would be quickly forgotten once the members of the Resistance understood how one building would change history.

* * *

Humanity so blinded by the promise that the Pleth would restore their lost technology, chose to ignore the exclusion of females in their delegations and troops. They never delved into the details of the Pleth reproductive cycle, and how it required a female. If they had, humans would have asked where the females were, and the answer would have reminded them of their own history when slavery was a profitable business and women had no rights.

The Pletha are no more than living incubation machines for Pleth offspring. A lifespan of approximately four hundred years dedicated to providing children for the Pleth. Children are torn from their mothers' arms shortly after birth so the Pletha can once again fulfill their role.

Unlike the Pleth, we Pletha do not have ear slits. Other than our two hearts, you cannot tell us apart from female humans. And like your females, we rebelled. We will not let the Pleth determine our existence any longer. The culture of reproduction needs to change, and we are willing to end our species' existence if it doesn't happen. We are walking among you. We fight beside you. And we will not let the Pleth win.

It doesn't matter if you're human or Pletha; we're on the same side. If you are reading this info-slide, it means there is hope. You have been curious enough to risk your life to seek this place of power, and smart enough to know its worth. Don't be discouraged that there's nothing left. We took it all.

The Library lives again. Its strength will help humanity triumph, and the Pletha escape their shackles.

Learning From Your Library

by Mohamed Abdi

Mohamed Abdi is a Somali-Canadian Writer with a Bachelor's Degree in Communication Studies. He loves to read mystery and historical fiction novels and has written articles for both online and print magazines. Mohamed lives in Edmonton with his wife and children.

It was a beautiful summer day and Gudal Haji-Ali was off from his night shift. Since he'd arrived in Canada and landed directly in Edmonton, a year and a half ago, he hadn't visited any library, though he adored books. He had too many commitments and his time was very tight. He worked six days a week and rarely had any social or leisure activities. He'd left his parents and siblings in a refugee camp in Kenya, which bordered his native Somalia. He'd begun sending remittance to his family the instant he started working at a shipping and receiving company in Edmonton. The job was very difficult for him, but he endured it to sustain him and his family.

One rare afternoon of calm free time, he strolled from his downtown Edmonton apartment to Stanley Milner Library to see for himself what was there, and to get connected with the library.

Gudal Haji-Ali opened the two sets of doors of the Stanley

Milner Library and found himself amid people bustling in and out. On his right was a sign that read "Second Cup".

"What is second cup? I have not even had my first one," he whispered to himself. Under the sign stood two pictures of full cups of coffee, and on a gray wall facing him hung a black artificial clock, which in place of the numbers and hands read "Time for Great Coffee."

He hesitated as to whether he should proceed into the library or check out the cafe. He needed coffee, but had never been to Second Cup.

Stroking his trimmed beard, he looked at his left wrist to check the time. It was 1:00 p.m. and behind him not a single cloud marred the empty Sunday sky. He strolled into the café and paced up and down the length of its pastry counter, turning his head to peer into the shop's corners. He struggled to absorb the variety of offerings while customers came in one after another and formed a long line.

With both hands in his faded black jeans' pockets, he joined the queue and shuffled along. A couple ahead of him took a bit longer than other customers, and he could sense the growing impatience behind him. His own turn came much faster than he would have liked, however.

"Hi, what can I get for you?" asked a female barista.

Gudal looked down and saw that her nametag said 'Susie'. "I need a cup of coffee," he replied.

"What kind and size?" she asked.

"What kinds do you have?" he said, looking back at the other customers behind him. Some fidgeted; others were checking their phones. Gudal knew he was even slower than the couple ahead had been, and thought he was holding up customers.

"There is strong, light, etc.," said Susie the barista.

"Can I get a strong coffee?" he said, exhaling through a clenched jaw.

"Anything else?" she asked.

"No, thank you."

She handed him a black, medium-sized cup of coffee.

He stared down. "But I need milk and sugar in it," he demanded.

"Milk and sugar are over there, and you can serve yourself," she told him, pointing to a side table.

Clutching the cup, he moved to another corner and felt overwhelmed again by the number of options in front of him. There were several labeled jars and a myriad of sticks, lids and packets. One jar's label read "half milk half cream". Rolling his sleeves up, he picked up the jar and poured some of its contents into his black coffee.

He made it overflow, and felt his cheeks flush. He grabbed napkins and padded down the counter, then wondered how he could carry the cup with hot liquid up to the brim. He dashed back to the counter.

"Can I get an empty cup, please?" he asked with a shy smile.

"Here you go," said a male barista who looked briefly at him, wondering what Gudal would do with the empty cup.

Gudal poured the excess into the empty cup, exhaling loudly. He began searching for a lid and sugar to sweeten his coffee.

After sweating through a search of dozens of packets at the side table, Gudal sweetened his coffee and managed to find a lid for his cup. Lifting his chest in triumph, he took a sip from the cup, but the coffee was cold; he had put more milk than he'd needed.

"It's spoiled," he muttered, trying to avoid destructively squeezing the cup. He ran one hand through his thick afro hair, shaking his head, and went towards the library, where he should have gone in the first place.

Gudal stepped onto the library's main floor with the intention of exploring different corners of it. He stopped in the open atrium and was surprised by the number of people milling around of all ages and backgrounds. Three security guards in black uniforms, one female and two males, walked in different directions up and down the main floor. The female security guard had a walkie-talkie in her hand and was talking soundlessly into it.

As though following the security guards' pattern, Gudal walked back and forth for about ten minutes, reading the posters and signs and watching people and their interactions. They were almost as diverse as the books lining the shelves. Eventually, he approached the library's membership service area and waited in line for his turn.

"How can I help you?" asked a bespectacled female librarian with cropped blonde hair.

"Can I get a library card?" he said.

"Sure, you can," she replied. "Do you have two pieces of ID on you?" Gudal pulled out a black wallet, then took out an operator's license and another identification card.

"Have you had a library card before?" asked the librarian.

"No, this will be my first one," he said.

"Your first one is free; you don't have to pay anything."

She smiled, and brought out a colourful assortment of cards, each with a different slogan in white lettering. "You can have any one of these."

He took off his silver framed eyeglasses and smiled. "Thank you. That is great." He chose a green card with a slogan "This card makes you smart."

He held the card delicately in his hands. Gudal wanted to become a smart man, of course.

"The library card lets you checkout 40 items at a time, ranging from books to magazines to DVDs and the like," said the librarian.

Gudal's eyes widened and he stared down at the green card. He inserted it gingerly into his wallet, knowing that such a powerful yet small card would prove immeasurably useful. As he left the desk, he smiled and gave a quick wave to the blonde woman, whom he thought might be reluctant to shake hands.

Moving farther into the library to browse, he saw patrons self-checking out items and wondered if he had to do the same. However, he put aside his worries, took a deep breath, and proceeded to wade through the library.

Sizing up stacks of books and adjusting his eyeglasses now and then, he strolled between shelves on spotless carpet. All the shelves were filled to the top. He followed a sign that read "General Fiction" in an easterly direction, knowing that if he lost his bearings he might never get out. He kept scanning book spines until he reached the farthest corner of the general fiction section. He furrowed his brow as he tried to return by the same path. He began to notice other sections with signs that read "Science Fiction", "Mystery", while another one indicated "Romance". The mystery section grabbed his attention, so he ducked between the shelves and started pulling off titles haphazardly.

Two years of working in a medium-sized library of a Somali Ministry of Commerce had given Gudal surprisingly little knowledge of library science. He was 19 years old when he got that job, almost four years ago. He could not go to university due to poor high school grades and a lack of money with which to bribe the university administration, so he had to look for work to get by. He was eventually successful landing the library job through one of his uncle's connections.

As time went by, the library's manager liked Gudal's work ethic and enthusiasm. As a result, he was sent to two library-related local workshops. Gudal liked his job, although he would have preferred to be in university. Most of his old classmates were studying different disciplines at the university by then. Gudal was disheartened whenever he encountered them, carrying heavy textbooks and bragging about their respective fields of study.

Throughout high school, Gudal had worked in a restaurant part-time to supplement his family's income. His older brother only completed the intermediate grade levels and became a truck driver. He could only support his family, as he was a married man with three children—nothing was left over for Gudal's parents and other siblings.

Gudal's three younger sisters had still been in school when he'd worked at the library. Their father, Haji-Ali, was the family's breadwinner. He'd been an employee of a post office for more than two decades and was well-known throughout the town. Gudal had been working in the library for two years when Somalia's civil war changed everything.

In Gudal's view, the Stanley A. Milner Library he was in now and the one he had worked for before he got displaced were incomparable—not even the same species. One was sophisticated and modern, the other small and primitive.

It took him a long time to choose a book. He would pick one up, read its title, open it briefly, read a line or two and put it back. Only in the mystery section did he hold onto books for a bit longer. He continued a bit more slowly, then stopped completely—his gaze fixated on the thrilling mystery in his hands. He raised his eyebrows and stuffed the book quickly under his armpit, as if someone else might take it.

"This is a wonderful book," he said.

He continued browsing for more interesting titles, found another book, then another. Each time the choice became easier. Now he had three candidates for signing out. He knew he could take out forty books if he wanted, but nevertheless put one of them back and headed for the library's main desk. He felt tired from the lengthy walk between the stacks, but thought it was worth the trouble.

The same bespectacled librarian who had received him when he'd first come in checked out the two novels for him.

"These are nice novels, eh?" she said.

"Thank you," Gudal replied.

Then he departed with two thick mystery novels, each one containing more than 350 pages. Gudal did not drive, although he had a license, but was okay with taking buses whenever he wanted to. He shared a two-bedroom apartment with a middle-aged man from his own community. Unlike Gudal, his apartment-mate was a married man, but like Gudal, had also left his family back in Kenya. Gudal worked in a warehouse; his roommate worked in a Fort McMurray camp. However, he would come to Edmonton for only a few days every three weeks, so Gudal was alone most of the time.

He walked back to his apartment feeling like he'd raided a tomb of secret knowledge. With his left hand holding the two thick novels, he took out his keys and opened his unit.

"Asalaamu Alaikum, Mukhtar," Gudal greeted.

"Wa alaikuma saalam," Mukhtar replied.

"How are you?" Gudal plunged himself onto a sofa and gasped for air. "It is very hot in here. Are the windows closed?" Not waiting for an answer, he stood up and checked them. Then he plugged in a fan for more circulation.

"Have you ever been to downtown Edmonton library?" Gudal asked.

"No," said Mukhtar. "What do they have there?"

"Everything you can think of—books, magazines, DVDs—lots of things. These people must love to learn."

Gudal lay down on his back, tucked a pillow under his head, stretched out his legs and began reading one of the novels. "Can you reduce the volume?" he said, motioning to Mukhtar who was sitting in front of a TV set.

Mukhtar fiddled with the remote control. "Is that okay?"

"Yes," Gudal said, distracted. He continued reading, satisfied that he could read pages and pages without encountering any vocabulary that hindered his comprehension. As time drew on though, he came across a few words obscure

107

to him. He grabbed a notepad and jotted the words down to look up in a dictionary that was beside him on a table. Oxford English Dictionary was Gudal's best companion, and he always had a copy near or with him.

The dictionary was all marks and explanations. Gudal would not only learn the meanings of new words, but he could follow the dictionary's proper pronunciation. Indeed, he had a passion for English and was adamant to improve it. His English skills had drastically advanced during his stay in Kenya as a refugee. He'd spent a lot of his spare moments on his favourite pastime: reading, specifically reading inexpensive novels he got from a second hand bookshop in Nairobi, Kenya's capital. Gudal was also a member of the British consulate in Nairobi, so he would often borrow books from there.

He loved the language and its powerful influence. In fact, Gudal's interest in English began in his elementary years when his uncle bought him a second hand English beginner book. Gudal's uncle was a highly-regarded high school teacher who taught English.

Very quickly, Gudal had realized that Somali and English were written in the same way. This revelation came after looking at book one of the "Oxford for Africa" volume his uncle bought him. The "Oxford for Africa" was a set of six books filled with a great deal of knowledge, if a person could complete the entire set. At long last, Gudal did just that while in Somalia, but he was still not proficient in English until he came to Kenya.

Gudal loved both libraries and books. Nevertheless, that passion was disrupted when he came to Canada due to a busy schedule and overwhelming commitments. He worked a nine-hour night shift six days a week in a warehouse. That didn't leave him much of anything, much less time for reading or visiting libraries. He had to provide for his entire family back in the refugee camp in Kenya.

The following week, Gudal returned to the library. It was another beautiful, cloudless Sunday afternoon. Upon entering, he proceeded to the Second Cup. Unlike the previous time, he confidently ordered his drink and put in the correct amount of sugar and milk. This time, he was well-dressed and had shortened his thick afro hair. Scanning the corners of the cafe, he spotted a vacant chair and hastened to claim it. With a hot cup of coffee in his hand, he sat down, unbuttoned and removed his black suit jacket, and smiled, feeling at peace in the place which before had seemed so alien. Seated at the table next to him were a man and a woman side-by-side at a computer, taking turns searching the Internet. They would type phrases, await answers, then burst out in laughter.

"They must be having fun," he thought. Although he was not intending to eavesdrop, his attention was forcefully attracted by their continual laughter.

One time, the young man stared at Gudal, making him look away and shift uncomfortably in his seat. With his cup of coffee nearing its end, Gudal stood up, took a big gulp, and threw the empty cup into the garbage can next to his table.

He bypassed the library's main desk this time and headed to the fiction section, which seemed to call out to him. He could not ignore the urge to revisit it after how captivating he'd found it the last time. Once again, he found himself leisurely walking between stacks of books, scanning categories and titles. Without committing to any book he found, he ended up in a magazine section adjacent to the fiction section.

"Magazines are shelved alphabetically," read a sign.

Gudal was enthralled, and stared wide-eyed around the section at its neat organization. One magazine's heading grabbed his attention, and he was soon flipping through its pages.

"25 years of Canadian Police in the Pursuit of Peace."

He left with the magazine and sat in a sofa near a window. He continued flipping pages and looking at the neatly framed pictures inside.

One news story's title read "Nation Mourns Slain Mounties", and started off with, "On June 4, 2014, the following three individuals died while on duty in Moncton, N.B. (New Brunswick).

Gudal wondered how they had died, and who had killed them. His heart grew heavy when he thought of the slain soldiers' loved ones. The incident reminded him of Somalia's gruesome civil war and all the families ravaged by it. He read on, turning the pages a bit more slowly.

A little later, he vacated the seat, leaving the magazine lying there. He went to another isle and saw many more magazines with captivating colours and titles. He started flipping through another magazine when a female library page pushing a trolley burdened with books passed by him. She wore a white T-shirt and black pants.

Gudal waved to get her attention and said, "Hi, excuse

me."

She didn't respond to him, but instead pointed at her ears and shook her head.

Gudal assumed she meant, "I am deaf and cannot hear you." He nodded back at her, lowering his hand. His question could wait.

Gudal left the main floor and climbed a marble staircase to the second floor. There he began to wade through a multitude of resources—not just the books he'd expected . The floor was replete with computers busied by all sorts of customers. This floor seemed even bigger than the first floor. His eyes caught big numeric signs while he roamed:

200 religions, 300 social science, 400 language, 500 science, 600 technology. These numbers reminded him of the two library workshops he had received during his employment in Somalia. After seeing those numbers, vague memories of the Dewey decimal system flashed back into his mind. It was something he had heard about but never memorized during those library workshops so long ago.

As there were many workstations on the second floor, he took up one workstation and got the attention of a librarian who was nearby, asking for help with how to log on.

"How can I use this computer?" Gudal asked.

"Oh, what do you want to use?" asked the librarian.

"I need the Internet."

"Are you logged on?" said the librarian.

Gudal was not yet logged on, but did not want to seem like a new member.

"Oh, you are right, so I have to first log in?"

The librarian understood that Gudal was new to the

library, and did not ask anything further.

Gudal followed the man's polite instructions and found himself staring at a desktop of icons.

"Now you can select what you want from here. You have numerous choices: Word, Internet Explorer, Acrobat Reader, etc.," said the librarian.

All that Gudal knew was how to use the Internet, since he had a desktop, and Google was his favorite search engine.

"Are you looking for anything in particular?" the librarian asked.

"I want to get books about the history of libraries," replied Gudal.

"Oh, then we can search them in the catalogue. Let's switch to that computer."

Gudal followed the librarian and watched him type up phrases and titles.

"You have all these books available here. Do you want me to write them down for you?"

"Yes, please," Gudal said.

The librarian put several titles on small pieces of paper and led Gudal through the stacks to an adjacent set of shelves.

"You can find all these books somewhere here; this is their section," said the librarian, glancing at Gudal who was walking slowly.

"Okay. I see," said Gudal.

The librarian continued along, pointing for Gudal's benefit, then pulled out three books and handed them to him. Gudal took them and looked at their titles, one by one.

"Do you need more?" asked the librarian.

"No, it is okay, thank you," replied Gudal.

Gudal returned to his workstation and studied the books' titles again.

One was "The Story of Libraries from the Invention of Writing to the Computer Age". He read the book's preface and scanned its contents.

All the chapters intrigued him. However, he put it down and began surfing the Internet before turning any more of its pages or looking at the other two books.

He googled "History of Libraries" and got back several hits, but clicked on one that interested him the most. Gudal read a long Wikipedia article about the history of libraries. One clause of the article defined a library as "…an organized collection of sources of information and similar resources, made accessible to a defined community for reference or borrowing".

He was scrolling up and down pages and reading that statement again and again, but the word "collection" was obscure to him. Consequently, he looked it up online and found its succinct meaning: "A collection is an aggregation of physical and/or electronic items".

This definition dispelled Gudal's uncertainty. He stumbled on another statement of the Wikipedia article saying, "A library's collection can include books, periodicals, newspapers, manuscripts, films, prints, documents, microform, CDs, cassettes, videotapes, DVDs, audiobooks, etc."

With his eyes fixed on the computer, Gudal wrapped his hands behind his neck and stretched. Instead of holding the mouse again, he picked up one of the books laying on his left and read its title, "Introduction to Cataloging and Classification."

"This is another good book," he mumbled to himself.

His gaze wandered briefly around the floor, and he stared at different patrons engaged in varied activities, some of whom were chatting. He intended to leave, but decided to stay a bit to surf the Net and glean a bit more about libraries and their evolution. He looked up library-related phrases and terms again, and each search yielded many results—almost too many. Furthermore, and to his surprise, the articles he found were in plain English and easy to comprehend. No complex vocabularies, no idioms, just plain language. He looked forward to reading more.

Gudal learned that libraries originated in Mesopotamia, which is modern-day south Iraq; he also learned that clay tablets and papyrus plants contributed to the first libraries. He was flabbergasted at how libraries had mutated from such a primitive state to where they were today. He discovered the interest people had in libraries increased significantly between 1600 and 1700, the era called "the Golden Age of Libraries".

He eventually logged out and left for the main desk to sign out the three books and head home. Gudal descended, following the marble stairs. He stood behind a male patron wearing wrinkled pants with a brown backpack dangling from his shoulder. The patron was speaking with one of the main desk library clerks.

"Do you have holds for me?" he asked.

"What is your name?" asked the clerk. After the man mentioned his name, she said, "Certainly, I have two set of books just for you." Shortly after, she handed him two full, white plastic bags of books.

Gudal was standing there, waiting for his turn to get the clerk's help. Meanwhile, he was astounded at how many books the patron was checking out. *How on earth he could read all those books?* Gudal thought. He recalled his first day at the library and what the bespectacled librarian told him pertaining to the power of his library card. Now he was seeing a practical example unfolding in front of him, someone signing out as many as 40 books.

Gudal came home with three nonfiction books in a green plastic bag. Nobody was at home, for Mukhtar had gone back to Fort McMurray.

Gudal switched on his television set and watched the news: local, national and international. His mind drifted while he watched until his cell phone rang and awoke him from his stupor. He lowered the volume, walked to a nearby table and answered.

"Hello, who is this?" he asked.

"It is Ahmed Farah," said Gudal's friend on the other end. "Are you at home?"

"Yes, I am at home," Gudal replied.

"I am coming to you."

"Sure, please come," Gudal said.

Ahmed arrived shortly thereafter. Gudal barely had enough time to clean up, but soon they were sitting side by side on the sofa drinking water and making small talk. Eventually Gudal had to share his latest discoveries, so he went and grabbed a few books from a small red wooden shelf. He put them on the coffee table in front of Ahmed.

"These books are wonderful," Gudal said. "I got them from Stanley A. Milner Library, this downtown one. Do you have a library card?"

"No, I do not," said Ahmed.

Gudal stood up, entered his room and came back with the tiny green card.

"This is the library card, and it is a powerful one because it enables you to borrow 40 items at once," said Gudal, observing his guest's expression.

"What would one person do with 40 items at once?" asked Ahmed.

"Well, I think Canadians like reading, and English is their language, after all," Gudal said.

"But 40 books are too many for just one person. How long does it take them to read all the 40 books?" he asked.

Gudal didn't have an answer, but instead picked up one of the fiction books he knew his friend would like. He summarized the plot. Ahmed was intrigued, so Gudal picked up another and another, relaying everything that was contained, and how the numbers on the spine corresponded to the book's contents.

"This is amazing," said Ahmed. "But I don't know if I could ever figure it all out."

"My friend," said Gudal, recognizing the overwhelmed sense of confusion in Ahmed's face, "let me take you to Second Cup, and I'll walk you through everything."

And they did. Before long Ahmed had a hot coffee, and his own library card that said, "What do you want to be today?"

When Gudal asked him the same question, Ahmed said he didn't know, but by the look in his eyes, Gudal sensed that the answer didn't matter as much as the available possibilities.

They reached the checkout counter and Gudal proudly gave his name.

"Certainly," said the clerk, turning to reach onto a shelf and retrieve a full plastic bag. "I have a set of books just for you."

Newcomers to Canada and Edmonton Public Libraries

by Trudie Aberdeen

Trudie Aberdeen is a long-time language educator and social justice advocate. She is currently working on completing her PhD on the topic of heritage language acquisition. In addition, she teaches English to adult newcomers to Canada. Her academic interests include refugee education, multilingual literacy instructional practices, language conservation, action research, and language instruction for heritage language learners. Her research can be found in the following journals: The Manitoba TEAL, Multilingual Discourses, and the 9th Low Educated Second Language and Literacy Acquisition (LESLLA) Symposium. She also serves as the book review editor to the Canadian Journal of Action Research.

Try to imagine what it would be like to be a poor, non-English-speaking, illiterate mother stuck inside an apartment with her children for three weeks during the holidays. Most of us can easily diagnose the cabin-fever and desperation that the Canadian winter and an apartment filled with bored children are about to induce. Now imagine this same mother taking her children to the library and showing them the books she desperately wants to be able to read herself. Imagine what it would feel like for this mother's mental health to be able to sit in a library, do the things that other Canadian mothers do—namely read to her children—and simply feel like an equal without having to say a word or spend a penny.

I work with a very specific sub-population of English as a second language (ESL) learners—illiterate adult refugees. Most of my students have never had the opportunity to attend school or were only allowed to attend it for a couple of years. Words often used to describe my students are poor, female, refugee, and mother. Almost all of my students have experienced some form of war, genocide, extended hunger or abuse. Despite whatever hardships they may have experienced in their previous lives, they were strong and organized enough to get their families and themselves into a refugee camp. When they feel safe enough to tell you, their stories of how they got to Canada are simultaneously terrifying and inspiring. Those who cannot recognize their strength call them victims. I call them survivors.

Many of my students never dreamed of coming to Canada. It was not their choice to come here, but rather an arbitrary decision made by some governing body at the United Nations. Many have told me that they would go "back home" if they could, but for them it is simply not possible. This does not mean that they don't love Canada; in fact, I have yet to meet a student who does not celebrate his or her life here. It's just that given the choice between a life where they can control and navigate their environment and be surrounded by friends and family or a life in Canada, perhaps unsurprisingly many would choose what they know. In their former countries they know how to operate electrical appliances, discipline their children without fear of someone calling social services, and buy a second-hand table without looking on Kijiji.

School and learning are very important for my students. As girls, many were either not allowed to attend, or the limited money was given to the boys instead. This is as true for my students who come from Afghanistan and Iraq as it is for my students who come from Nicaragua, China, Cambodia, Congo, Eritrea, Ethiopia and Laos. Contrary to the popular belief expressed in the media, uneducated girls are just as likely to be Christian, Buddhist or Atheist as they are Muslim. ESL classes for women who never got the chance to attend school as girls are more than just picking up some survival literacy—these classes represent a chance to experience school just like everyone else. The women rarely feel sad for what they never had, but rather are grateful that they finally get their turn!

Still, a life in Canada without formal education is not an easy one. Yes, a multitude of social benefits do exist to help those in need. Health care, Assured Income for the Severely Handicapped (AISH), Disabled Adults Transportation Service (DATS), welfare, Employment Insurance (EI), the Christmas Bureau, Child Tax Credit, subsidized housing, library cards, and Leisure Access Passes are a smattering of the offerings that Albertan society offers to those without means. Although my students and their families' daily lives are improved by financial support, their needs are far greater than the average Canadian can easily understand. For example, to access any of the supports mentioned in the list above requires that someone fill out a form listing basic information such as name, address, marital status, phone number, and date of birth. Students in my class need to learn how complete basic tasks like this one. In fact, as a first step I have taught many refugees to write their own name and recognize it in print.

If the African saying that it takes a whole village to raise a child is true, then it must also be true that it takes a village of supports (educational, financial, emotional, social, and psychological) to help the most vulnerable feel safe. A teacher or a social worker cannot possibly be all things to all refugee mothers; an important part of a teacher or social worker's job is helping students access others in the community who can help them. The Edmonton Public Library has been fundamental in its support of ESL learning, and refugee mothers. Usually twice a year, a librarian will come to my school to speak to the students about getting a library card. In addition to giving a presentation targeted at the appropriate English level, the librarian also meets one-on-one with the students and helps them apply for a library card by assisting them in completing the form.

For someone from Canada, filling out an application form for a library card might seem like a mundane task, but for my students it means that they had to talk to a Canadian (who wasn't their teacher), answer personal information questions, and fill out a real-world form to get something that would benefit them. Students know they are successful when they walk away with their own library card, a plastic piece of self-esteem that fits into a wallet.

The librarians at Edmonton Public Libraries do far more than hand out cards at these presentations, they also begin an important discussion about financial literacy. Most of my students are hopeless when it comes to managing money and understanding finances. They usually come from a place where either a husband or a father makes financial decisions or they work as day labourers. Women are rarely trusted with large sums of money to manage. In their former lives, when my students had their own money to buy something, they went to a market and negotiated a price. In Canadian stores, there is hardly any negotiating and little bartering. Here we find the best price through coupons, on-line deals, flyers, and discount cards. Again, each of these money saving options requires literacy and an ability to compare and price match, an academic skill my students never were taught.

It is very easy to fall into a bad financial place in Canada. Credit card debt, $3 fees to use an ATM, bank overdraughts and payday loans are but a few ways one can destroy herself financially. When Edmonton Public librarians visit ESL classes to tell students about the services offered at the library, they introduce key concepts which help refugees become socialized into the Canadian way of doing things. Even something as simple as learning how a book scanner works may teach someone from a cash-only society how to use an automated check-out or an ATM machine. Edmonton Public librarians also explain concepts like library fees for overdue materials and how multiple unpaid fines can affect one's credit rating. While some might consider this a bit of a "lecture", for low-literate refugees this talk represents an introduction into the complex world of financial literacy. These learners can find out some of the unpleasant conse-quences of unpaid bills before having to experience them first-hand. For almost all, it is a first exposure to the concepts of credit ratings and collection agencies. It is essential for newcomers to understand that simple choices that seem unconnected could have serious financial consequences for the future. This is a lesson that we hope new Canadians get before they get their first "pre-approved" credit card application or take out a loan for furniture with 28% interest.

Loneliness is a serious problem for many of these women. Although refugee camps are not regarded as desirable locations or long-term habitations, when these women are relocated to Canada, they are taken away from their social networks and for the first time many are without friends. Some are actually fearful to leave their homes because they are worried about getting lost, making a social faux-pas, not having someone to talk to, getting duped into spending money they don't have, and not being able to follow someone's instructions and, as a result, looking foolish. Once they have met a librarian and received a library card, they feel more confident walking into the library. Being in a shared space allows them to make friends and helps them re-establish some of the social networks that were lost. The mothers can attend puppet shows or story time with their babies. They can sit in a room and feel a part of something even if they cannot understand the language. They can sit beside their children who are using the computer and maybe make small talk with the mom beside them. Having an inexpensive and welcoming place to go, especially one where you can bring your children, is essential to mental health for many. Making new friends and social connections means keeping one's mental health. For some refugee mothers, this is everything.

This loneliness is usually compounded by the fact that these women lose the ability to talk to their children. It usually happens so quickly that families do not see it coming. Once the children start school, their lives become awash in English, and they often experience a drought of their first language. Children are motivated to learn English so that they can be academically successful, have friends, watch TV, use the computer, and play at the park with the other kids. The mothers do not learn at the same speed. Usually within a year, the child's mother tongue becomes limited to transactional and receptive language, while their English flourishes. The same is not true for the mothers who struggle to learn basic concepts without being able to take notes. While this abandoning of one's first language for English has some benefits for the child's schooling, it is devastating for the family. Once the children lose their parents' language, they often lose their values, their histories, and their traditions.

The only way to prevent language loss is to help parents teach their children. Librarians can and often do play a pivotal role in helping family members communicate with one another. Not only do Edmonton's libraries provide spaces for language classes, they house books, music, videos, and resources in languages other than English. Librarians often put these materials in the hands of the refugee mothers so they can share them with their children. Even if the mothers are unable to read the contents, they still have a concrete object they can use to springboard into a conversation about their country of origin. The children become exposed to new vocabulary and ideas which further language acquisition while the mother shares some of her experiences, values, and knowledge with her children. In this way children shift their perception of their mother as someone who cannot do many things to someone who is capable and intelligent about things that they know little about. Librarians do not just connect patrons with books; they connect patrons with each other, too.

The Edmonton Public Libraries have a cache of treasured English language learning materials. Finding reading material for adults with little or no experience with print is challenging, but for my level of language learners the Edmonton Public Libraries have simplified readers which use easy vocabulary and only have one sentence per page. These readers are not readily available in bookstores and learners would have to know how to order them in a bookstore in order to purchase them. Believe it or not these simplified readers often cost as much as $15 each, making them too expensive for my learners to buy for themselves. In addition to having these books available, learners can also borrow picture dictionaries, books on tape and children's books. These materials are very expensive for a cash-strapped struggling family. Without access to these materials from the public library many mothers and children would not have any access to them at all.

The fact that our libraries have collections of books is surprising to no one, but the fact that they have such extensive collections in languages other than English is. Edmonton Public Libraries have materials in over 40 languages, subscribes to over 800 international newspapers, and even has a Chinese magazine database! They literally carry Amharic to Xhosa! Can you imagine how such small pieces of your former home: such as newspapers, children's and adults' books, videos and music, magazines,

CDs and DVDs, can make you feel more comfortable in your new one? Expensive telephone calls are often the only way that illiterate adults can get access to information about their homeland. However, librarians are willing to show these women how to use the internet to look up images on google maps, call their relatives on Skype, or find videos on YouTube. While some might be able to ask their children to help them find this information, it shifts the balance of the mother-child relationship towards the child and is dependent on the patience of the "teacher". Librarians help my students to find the information they seek and to become self-reliant in finding answers to their own questions.

Another way in which refugee mothers become self-sufficient is by working. Being able to provide for their children is a preoccupation for these women. Librarians will work with my students and help them look for jobs, create simple résumés, fill in job application forms, and fax or email them to potential employers. To complete any of these tasks requires technical know-how. Librarians are always willing to assist someone meet their personal goals. This means helping someone learn how to use a computer, photocopier or fax machine. Librarians often help refugee mothers find their first Canadian jobs. There was a well-known bumper sticker in the 70s that said "If you can read this, thank a teacher!" On a similar note, you might want to thank a librarian at an Edmonton Public Library if:

- you are a refugee to Canada who can get help learning English or learning to read;

- you have a safe, low-cost place to take your children so that you can connect with them better;

- you don't feel isolated and know where you can make friends with other Canadians;

- you can gather news and current events about your home country;

- you can find language materials to help you keep the lines of communication open with your family, both here and overseas;

- you can get access to English learning materials;

- you can access support in operating technology;

- you've learned about how money works in Canada;

- you've increased self-esteem because you learned how to do things for yourself;

It just doesn't fit as nicely on a bumper sticker.

Reading After Hours

by Hal J. Friesen

Hal writes science fiction, plays at science for a living, and studies cello. He wore an astronaut costume for 167 days in a contest to go to space. He grew up in Prince George, BC, and holds a BSc in Chemistry and Physics, and MSc in Electrical Engineering. Now working as a Research Scientist in laser gas detection, he spends his working hours making and breaking new concepts, before going home to unleash his imagination writing on a homemade treadmill desk. He lives in Edmonton with a gnome painted like Super Mario.

———————

S helves seemed to lean and watch Albert stride down the hallway toward the public washroom. The pressure in his groin readied to break and gush into his pants, which would make for a long evening of studying. He wished he could force himself to care about such mundane nuisances as bodily excretions, but most of the time the processes got in the way of his real work.

Some of the lights turned off as Albert approached the bathroom. The librarians tended to cut power to some book sections as day drew into evening and the scraped shelves got a respite from the steady stream of students. Albert had tuned everything out in order to concentrate in what was supposed to be a quiet haven: he'd even tuned out his own body.

The short brown carpet was hardly better than the concrete beneath. Albert considered himself a silent walker, but the sound in the library had been sucked up so completely that all he could hear were his padding feet. The shadows seemed darker in the gaps between the bookshelves, the spaces narrower.

Albert shoved the bathroom door open, the valve in his pants beginning to unseat in anticipation. He groaned when he saw one urinal occupied, the other out of order. He stumbled into the nearest stall, banging the door open. Albert slammed it shut and latched it, yanked down his pants and fell onto the toilet seat. He closed his eyes as he drained his bladder, sighing.

The other occupants had long since vacated by the time Albert stood, pulled up his pants and reached for the handle to flush. Carved and handwritten musings of other patrons surrounded the white porcelain. The writings declared profound iconoclastic tendencies or merely asserted the existence of genitalia, a need Albert found exceedingly common. He pushed the toilet handle down, readying for the cleansing water from the spattered rim.

BANG!

Albert barely had time to shield his face from the flying shards. He fell back against the bathroom door. The water—his own—sprayed up and all over him. It was all over in a moment, and Albert stared down at the shattered toilet seat as drops of blood and urine trickled onto the tiled floor. Sharp jets of pain shot up from the edges of his hand. His ears echoed with the siren of the blast. He stared at the scene, tasting the putrid liquids he had been so determined to avoid by coming to the washroom. He could only think how grateful he was to have drunk the spoilt milk that morning that had voided his bowels earlier rather than now.

Albert winced when he pulled the stall door open. He stumbled out and bent over the sink, seeing that hand was sliced up in several places. Thankfully none of the cuts were very deep. Gritting his teeth, he turned on the tap and watched as water sputtered out between jets of air. He surmised that must have been the problem that had cracked the porcelain—air in the water lines. A great, little-known problem of centralized toilets. He washed his hands and sponged off his face with his uninjured hand.

It would be harder to concentrate on electrical concepts with a lame hand, and even worse, he thought, after the wasted time spent explaining what had happened. The toilet's explosion had been as loud as a bomb, and without a doubt a horde of angry librarians would be in any minute to tell Albert to quiet down.

But no one came. By the time Albert had rinsed his shirt off and crept back into the library, the lights were off. The only sound he could hear was a faint whistle as though a crack in a window were letting in the crisp winter air. The trickle of illumination from the washroom snuffed out as the door shut behind Albert.

He was not a superstitious person. His father and mother were both non-observant Ashkenazi Jews, and he was even less observant, if that were possible. There was nothing that couldn't be explained by the power of deductive reasoning. Scientific logic precluded the existence of the occult, and Albert's hoped-for mastery of deduction was one of the reasons he was out studying when everyone else had gone to bed.

Nevertheless, the small hairs on his arms stood at attention, as rigid as the conscripts he'd avoided joining by renouncing his citizenship. The library wasn't supposed to be closed this early, but without a watch Albert could only estimate the time. It had been around seven o'clock when he'd headed for the bathroom, a good two hours before closing time. There was no way he could have spent that long in there, no matter how pleasurable the release of bladder pressure.

The way back to his library stall was obscure, and in the dimness the shelves looked like they'd rearranged themselves to make a maze. He told himself not to be ridiculous, waited a moment for his eyes to adjust, then walked forward.

The floor creaked and the shelves swayed with each step. He reached the end of the 'M' book section and turned to go along the corridor between the ribs of bookshelves. He heard a thump, and turned to see a book lying open on the carpet, its pages creased from the impact. Albert looked both ways, wondering if this was all a practical joke by his cruel classmate, Franz.

Albert tasted the cold dry air, trying to quiet his breathing. He clenched his fists and bent down, looking all around him. He gingerly grabbed the book, turned it and squinted in the dimness to read the cover. Science and Hypothesis, by Henri Poincare. The page was opened to a preface that read, "To doubt everything or to believe everything are two equally convenient solutions; both dispense with the necessity of reflection."

Albert frowned, checking his surroundings once more. Maybe this was Franz's handiwork. The ex-friend knew more about Albert than he liked; enough to hit him where it hurt. Albert hardly thought he doubted everything—just some of the theories with gaps in understanding. He shut the book with a resounding thunk and set it at the side of the shelf. A librarian could put it back in its proper place later. Albert had more important things to do, and whoever Mr. Poincare was could wait. He would find Franz, throttle him, then get back to his studies.

When Albert turned he heard another thump behind him. The same book had fallen down again, this time to another page: "As we can not give a general definition of energy, the principle of the conservation of energy signifies simply that there is something which remains constant."

If I don't get back to my desk to study, Albert thought, the only constancy will be my employ as a factory worker. "All right," Albert said, "stop this nonsense, Franz. I know you're there."

There was no reply. Usually when given the satisfaction of acknowledgment, Franz would have sniggered or chortled, Albert was sure of it. The faint, distant whistle of air wasn't something Albert would have attributed to the traitorous friend.

He left the book on the floor and started ahead, swinging his arms for momentum. There's nothing to be afraid of, he told himself. Books shifted, and that's all there is to it. Coincidences can create what appears to be miraculous intervention.

He steeled himself by picturing the hard-headed Mrs.

Spiegel scolding him for not following the regimented method of solving circuit problems. She had no ideas concerning the ether which might permeate everything and dictate every law that drove electrical charges in their circuit merry-go-rounds. She was there for the bottom line, and had no time for the introspection that would push under-standing closer to the mind of the universe. Albert wouldn't give Franz the satisfaction of seeing him embarrassed in front of the whole class.

Albert passed closer to the mathematics section, which gave him hope he was close to his destination. The sound of his heart quieted in his ears as he surrounded himself by the crisp tomes of logicians and mathematikers. Albert halted just in time as a book nearly landed on his head. Its spine cracked on the hard floor with a sickening crunch. Albert yelped as the page groaned open onto his shoe to a theorem derivation. He jerked his foot away and took a few deep breaths.

It was an algebra book, and the theorem was one by Emma Noether.

Noether, he thought. No. Ether.

"I must be really trying to convince myself not to study," he said, louder than he really needed to. "I know I don't like Mrs. Spiegel, but she's a stepping stone to greater things. Come on Albert, let's forget this nonsense."

He continued on and halted when the way was blocked by a shelf jutting perpendicular to all the others. Albert was certain the placement hadn't been that way earlier, and the lay of the bookshelves looked suddenly unfamiliar. Franz was clever and industrious in his scheming ways, but not that clever. The encroaching walls of books seemed closer, sanctuary ever farther.

He swallowed. "That's all right," he said, voice shaking. "Some last-minute reshuffling to make room for more books." The words seemed to be pushed back at him by the chill air, dying before they even made it to the books.

Another tome fell beside him, and he jumped back against the opposite bookshelf. He squinted and saw that it was open to another theorem by Noether.

Albert squeezed his eyes shut, wishing he could be non-observant right now. When he opened them again and saw the book still lying there, he found himself wanting Franz to jump out of the shadows and make everything real again. The words formed on his lips before he could think them through. "Are you... the ghost of Emma Noether?"

Another book fell down, louder, as though the building shouted in response. It was "Principles of the Dynamics of the Electron" by Abraham.

Electrons are negatively charged, Albert thought, turbidity rising in his stomach. Does that mean no?

"So you're not the ghost of Emma Noether," he said, eyes searching for a source. The books behind jutted hard into his back. He cried out and lurched free of their touch. "I'm having a dream then," he said between gasps of air. He was almost shouting now, as though the words could push away the darkness. "I must have dozed off at my desk, and now I'm bending reality with my... nonlucid mind."

The shelves creaked and groaned. A rumbling started in the distance. Albert shuffled back and almost tripped. He turned in every direction. He couldn't—he mustn't—touch any more books. They fattened and leaned over him, making a tunnel above him. The rumble grew to a roar, and Albert froze at the sight of a wave of books pouring off the shelves as though the Earth had been split asunder.

Albert ran from the deafening sound. He wove through the rat maze of shelves, his skinny legs wobbling with every step. He was not built for a marathon, and prayed his body wouldn't figure it out as quickly as his mind had.

The passage ahead of him narrowed. Albert cried out. The locust thunder felt right behind his ears. Something caught his heel, and he tried to twist and right himself. A book caught his flailing arm and a great force slammed him face-first into the side shelf. There was a blinding flash of light, then Albert was swarmed by a tide of hardcover books, their spines opening and closing like shark jaws.

Air rushed out of Albert's lungs as the books piled higher and higher up his body. He tried to push back and away from the waterfall that was now moving so fast it might as well have been flowing water. But he couldn't move. He twisted his head away and winced, repeating to himself that there was nothing he could do now. His rational side fought hard to hold on as he clenched his jaw, readying himself for the hammering that would smash his skull in.

All at once, everything stopped. There was a great pause and Albert felt like the library took in a breath of air before a final thump hammered on his chest. He wheezed and coughed, daring to open an eye.

Propped open on his chest, still shaking from its energetic journey, was a thin and tall gray hardcover book with a white lettered title: "Let's Read Aloud". Beneath the title was a golden pictogram of vines and flowers entwining a wagon, a crown, an elephant and a unicorn.

Albert said nothing. The book rocked with the tremors of standing waves in the layers upon layers beneath it. Albert felt like any motion or noise might cause another torrent to fall and finish him off. He wondered if people buried up to their heads in the sand felt the same sense of overwhelming panic in every fragment of their bodies.

The air whistled loudly and the book quavered back and forth in front of Albert. The books suddenly felt like an enormous hand pinning him to the ground, and he whimpered at the realization of his own helplessness. He cried out, but that only made the shaking mass on top of him more violent.

"What do you want me to read aloud?!" Albert shouted, tears streaming down his cheeks.

Abruptly the tremors ceased. Albert heard and felt the thunderous shuffling of all the books on the entire floor—maybe even the entire building. A dark rectangle flew threw the air, angling straight for Albert's head—and landed right in front of him, the entire mass of books bucking and cradling the impact.

Albert looked through slitted eyes at the open brown pages in front of him. It seemed to be an archived collection of articles from Godey's Magazine, and the page was open to "LE MELANGE. Everything from the soil."

Albert scanned the first few phrases:

All the artists, manufacturers, and commercialists of the world are employed on the produce of the soil, and on that only. The watchmaker and the anchor-smith…

"I've gone insane," Albert said.

The library roared, the shelves leering down at him as waves smashed shelves far away. A book rolled into place in front of him, aided by the changing topography of the sea of written works.

The book fluttered open, and all Albert caught was the author: David Hume. Pages tore violently away, leaving a fluttering leaflet jutting out of the spine in the middle of untouched pages. The leaflet read:

No testimony is sufficient to establish a miracle, unless the testimony be of such a kind, that its falsehood would be more miraculous than the fact which it endeavors to establish.

Albert swallowed. "I don't know if I'd call this a miracle."

There was a flurry of motion, and Albert's whole body seemed ready to be bent in half by the current of books. When he settled down again, he was staring at another page of David Hume's work, but whether it was from the same book or another he couldn't be sure.

"A wise man proportions his belief to the evidence," Albert read aloud. "And there's a lot of evidence," he muttered. He looked around for where the next book might launch from, and tried unsuccessfully to take a deep breath, for the weight of all the books pressed tightly against his chest.

"Okay," he said, "you've given me enough evidence." He frowned, trying to think back. "You want me to read... Le Melange?" He tried and failed once more to move his body. "I read much better when I'm not being crushed."

The book tides roared and a copy of Charles Dickens's

Great Expectations opened up before Albert. "I am what you designed me to be," Albert read. "I am your blade. You cannot now complain if you also feel the hurt."

Albert's lips trembled. "W—what are you?"

Shelves rocked and swayed until Jane Austen's Pride and Prejudice planted itself within eyesight. "I cannot fix on the hour, or the spot, or the look or the words, which laid the foundation. It is too long ago. I was in the middle before I knew that I had begun."

The book did a flip and switched with the copy of Great Expectations, and Albert read on: "You are part of my existence, part of myself. You have been in every line I have ever read, since I first came here, the rough common boy whose poor heart you wounded even then. You have been in every prospect I have ever seen since—on the river, on the sails of the ships, on the marshes, in the clouds, in the light, in the darkness, in the wind, in the woods, in the sea, in the streets. You have been the embodiment of every graceful fancy that my mind has ever become acquainted with."

The book slammed shut and fell down as another catapulted into place, the cushioning action rocking Albert. It was Leo Tolstoy's Anna Karenina. "Not one word, not one gesture of yours shall I, could I, ever forget…"

Albert stared with wide eyes, waiting to see if there was more. When he could hear but a distant rumble of the bellows of the library breathing and beating the pulse of stored knowledge, he spoke a few barely audible words. "Are you going to kill me?"

The tome came faster, as though the library had had it at the ready: Middlemarch by George Eliot. "What loneliness is more lonely than distrust?"

Albert gulped. "Surely there must be a better way for us to… converse?"

Great Expectations hopped into place once more. "Scattered wits take a long time in picking up." The pages fanned into a blur as they shifted. "There was something very comfortable in having plenty of stationery."

Beneath the mountain of books that were piling up, Albert felt very stationary indeed. With the realization that he couldn't simply wait this out, he felt purpose stir within. "What do you want from me?"

It seemed more of the library's answers came from Dickens than anywhere else as Great Expectations opened once more. "There was a long hard time when I kept far from me the remembrance of what I had thrown away when I was quite ignorant of its worth."

"What is it you've lost?" Albert asked, his brow furrowed.

The pages flipped. "Pause you who read this, and think for a moment of the long chain of iron or gold, of thorns or flowers, that would never have bound you, but for the formation of the first link on one memorable day." Anna Karenina flipped in as soon as Albert had finished reading the words. "All the variety, all the charm, all the beauty of life is made up of light and shadow."

Albert felt desperation rise once more within him. "I don't understand you. These metaphors are too far removed from the topic you want to address."

Anna Karenina again. "For we all of us, grave or light, get our thoughts entangled in metaphors, and act fatally on the strength of them."

"What act can I take from all this?" Albert asked, voice rising. "What can I untangle from your references?"

A gold-embossed book with a drawing of a whale surged in front: Herman Melville's Moby Dick. "It is not down on any map: true places never are."

"You seek to show me some truth?"

A book on electricity—finally something relevant to what Albert sought, flipped in and opened to a page showing clouds of positive charges pushing away from each other.

"Yes?" Albert ventured.

Great Expectations kicked its way back in. "I looked at the stars, and considered how awful it would be for a man to turn his face up to them as he froze to death, and see no help or pity in all the glittering multitude."

"The truth is in the stars?"

Numerous books glided into place, all opening to mathematical theorems by Emma Noether.

"You suggest that there is no ether? That contradicts all common scientific wisdom."

George Eliot's Middlemarch careened back into view. "It is a narrow mind which cannot look at a subject from various points of view." Right after, Mark Twain's The Adventures of Huckleberry Finn replaced it. "Just because you're taught that something's right and everyone believes it's right, don't make it right."

Albert bit his lip, trying hard to be diplomatic. "What are the implications of this suggested universe without an ether?"

A rumbling wave had to reach far back into the annals of the library which seemed to Albert infinitely far away.

It was Mr. Poincare's book again, the same passage he'd read at the beginning of the night. "As we can not give a general definition of energy, the principle of the conservation of energy signifies simply that there is something which remains constant."

Albert groaned. "I can't get through this. I just wanted to study for my electronics exam."

Anna Karenina plopped again in front, in what seemed a circle of the library's favourite sources of wisdom. "Spring is the time of plans and projects."

"It's winter," Albert said miserably. Before he could add anything, numerous textbooks on electricity tumbled in a great waterfall, pushing away the ones beneath. The pages flipped open, beginning to turn methodically.

Albert tried to shake his head. "I can't take in information this way. There's too much." His eye caught one that was similar to his own textbook, and he tried to indicate it with a curt nod.

The library responded by showing him more and more, flipping to quizzes and questions Albert tried to answer while under the encumbrance of the world's weight of books. When he stumbled the library knew exactly what to bring out to elicit the clarity to push forward.

When Albert tried to argue his own point, the library would often retort with "You can't pray a lie," from Anna Karenina. Albert got stuck on a particularly challenging problem when light began to trickle in through the slits between the books. He blinked in surprise, astonished that so much time had passed. An icy hand gripped his heart as he realized he hadn't slept a minute the entire night, and he would have to face Franz and Mrs. Spiegel and the test with limited wits. The problem on the page in front of him seemed as intractable as everything else.

The library kept pushing the page closer, until it jammed into Albert's nose. Grunting, he stared once more at the figures, working his way through the derivations on his lips. Then all at once he got it, and shouted out the answer.

The library carried him in an undulating wave as a roar brought back Herman Melville's Moby Dick. "There she blows!—there she blows! A hump like a snow-hill! It is Moby Dick!"

Albert laughed and asked for his arms to be freed. The library obliged, carrying him like a sports champion. He closed his eyes, surprised the sea of hardcovers could be manipulated in a way that was cushioning and supportive.

Albert began to hear feet in the distance, and before he could say anything the library plopped him back on his feet, the books still swimming around him. Great Expectations opened again on a stationary island, opening slowly to the well-worn pages. "We changed again, and yet again, and it was now too late and too far to go back, and I went on. And the mists had all solemnly risen now, and the world lay spread before me."

Albert smiled. "We'll have to discuss more of your truths another night, when I don't have a test," he said. "So I will say goodbye for now, but it is a short goodbye."

The books parted around him, leaving the lonely island propping up the Dickens book. "Life is made of so many partings welded together." The books surged toward Albert once more, stopping just to touch both of his shoulders, then receded into the distance in a quieting thunder. Albert raised a hand and waved, but when he looked around the shelves were as they had been when he'd first come, before the toilet had exploded and the library had locked early to corner him. Before the notion of a universe with no ether, and suggestions of an unknown universal constant.

He patted a shelf after he'd collected his belongings, and headed to the door. Outside, he could see Mrs. Spiegel standing beside the school librarian waiting for her to open the library doors. Before Albert could dodge out of sight, they saw him. Soon he was standing face to face with two wrinkle-faced ladies frowning down at him.

"Mr. Einstein," Mrs. Spiegel said, "what in God's name are you doing hiding in the library?"

Made in the USA
Charleston, SC
13 March 2015